How to Turn Your Pet into an Instagram Star

Fame, Fortune, and Furry Friends

Andrea Johnson

SKAII PUBLISHING

Contents

Introduction

Welcome to "How to Turn Your Pet into an Instagram Star: Fame, Fortune, and Furry Friends". This book is a labor of love, born out of the delightful mix of the digital age and our age-old love for pets. Weaving together passion and practicality, it is designed as a short, well-structured guide to help you navigate the world of pet influencers on Instagram.

In the age of social media, our pets are no longer just our loyal companions; they can also be stars in their own right, garnering thousands, if not millions, of followers. As they bring joy, humor, and warmth into our lives, they also have the potential to do the same for a wider online audience.

This is not just a trend; it's a phenomenon that's growing every day.

This guide will walk you through every step of this fascinating journey - from identifying your pet's unique personality and building their brand, to growing their follower base and leveraging their fame for good causes. Each chapter dives into different facets of the pet influencer world, offering practical tips, strategies, and real-world examples to guide you through.

We cover everything from photography tips and writing engaging captions, to legal aspects, handling media attention, and dealing with challenges. Moreover, we delve into monetizing strategies and tips on how to expand your pet's online presence beyond Instagram.

However, this journey is not just about achieving fame or fortune. It's about celebrating the special bond we share with our pets, giving them a platform to shine, and connecting with a community that appreciates the unconditional love and joy pets bring into our lives.

As you flip through the pages of this guide, remember that every pet has a unique story to share with the world. Your role is to help them tell it. So, whether your furry friend is already a burgeoning Instagram star, or you're just starting out, this book is for you.

Let's embark on this exciting journey together, and turn the spotlight on our beloved pets. Let's create content that not only captures their adorable antics but also their unique personalities and charming hearts. Let's share their stories, one post at a time.

Welcome to the world of pet influencers. Let the journey begin!

CHAPTER ONE

Introduction to Pet Influencers

The Rise of Pet Influencers on Instagram

Pet influencers are not a new phenomenon, but the platform that has seen the greatest surge in their popularity in recent years is undoubtedly Instagram. Once a niche community, pet influencers have grown into an undeniable force in the world of social media, commanding millions of followers and striking lucrative brand deals.

The rise of pet influencers on Instagram has been propelled by the platform's unique focus on visual content and its user-friendly interface, which has opened up new opportunities for individuals to share the lives of their beloved pets with a global audience. From dogs and cats to parrots and hedgehogs, pets of all kinds have found a place in the Instagram limelight.

One of the key reasons for this rapid rise is the joy and positive emotions that pets naturally bring to people. Unlike human influencers who may bring with them an undercurrent of competition or envy, pets provide pure, unfiltered joy. Seeing a happy pet, engaged in playful antics or cuddled up in a cute pose, brings an immediate smile to people's faces, making pet profiles a hit among Instagram users.

In addition, Instagram has made it easy for people to discover new pet accounts. Features like the "Explore" page or hashtag searches enable users to find content that suits their interests. As a result, pets with distinctive features, special talents, or simply an engaging personality have found enormous audiences, some even surpassing human influencers in terms of follower counts and engagement rates.

Benefits of Having a Famous Pet

At first glance, the concept of a pet influencer may seem frivolous or even absurd, but there are tangible benefits to having a famous pet on Instagram. Here are a few:

1. Monetary Rewards: There is a fascinating and potentially highly lucrative facet to the world of pet influencers - the significant income they can generate through diverse revenue streams. This income is not negligible and has transformed into a major incentive for many pet owners to build their pets' online presence.

Among the most common and rewarding avenues for this income generation are brand partnerships. These collaborations involve pet influencers endorsing or promoting products from pet-centric businesses or even mainstream brands looking to tap into the burgeoning pet influencer market. This could range from pet food to toys to grooming products, and the range of items is only limited by the creativity of the brands involved.

Alongside brand partnerships, there's the avenue of merchandise sales. Pet influencers often have their own line of merchandise, including clothing, accessories, toys, and even their own branded food or treat ranges. With a dedicated and invested following, these items can sell in large numbers, driving a significant portion of the pet influencer's income.

Sponsorships represent another powerful income source for pet influencers. Companies pay to have their products or services featured or used by the influencer in their social media posts, videos, or during live events. This not only gives the brand exposure to a targeted demographic but also lends the credibility of the influencer to the brand, making it a win-win situation for both parties involved.

Lastly, but certainly not least, is advertising revenue. This is particularly relevant for pet influencers with popular YouTube channels or podcasts. Each view or listen can generate advertising revenue, and for the more popular channels, this can add up to a substantial sum. In some cases, popular pet influencers can make significant income from advertisements alone.

As the pet's popularity continues to escalate on these digital platforms, the potential for income growth expands exponentially. The more followers and engagement a pet influencer has, the more appealing they become to brands, advertisers, and sponsors. As a result, as the pet's fame grows, so too can the revenue it generates. It's not just a matter of scale but also the quality of the audience engagement that the pet can foster, driving loyalty and trust, which in turn can lead to higher profitability.

2. Charity and Advocacy: A notable attribute of having a famous pet is that it can be transformed into a powerful platform for advocacy and positive change. The broad reach of pet influencers in the digital sphere can be leveraged to make a tangible difference, and indeed, many do.

Numerous pet influencers and their human counterparts use their considerable influence and reach to illuminate critical issues related to animal welfare. They bring animal rights into the spotlight, creating dialogue around it. From discussions about appropriate care and ethical treatment to shining a light on the need for stronger legal protections, these influencers use their platforms to educate, inspire, and provoke thought among their followers.

Moreover, rescue and adoption efforts are also prominent themes that are often highlighted by pet influencers. They underscore the necessity of adopting pets from shelters, often sharing heartwarming stories of rescue animals that have found loving homes. Some pet influencers are rescue animals themselves, serving as living embodiments of the difference adoption can make. They also bring attention to the conditions many rescue animals live under, raising funds and mobilizing their followers to support rescue shelters and organizations.

Another critical aspect that pet influencers can spotlight are broader environmental issues. For instance, they can use their platform to highlight the impact of climate change on habitats and wildlife, or the issue of pollution, specifically plastic waste, which poses a threat to marine life. The connection between pets and broader environmental topics offers a relatable way for these influencers to engage their audience in discussions around environmental sustainability.

Moreover, pet influencers are often involved in charity work. They can host fundraising campaigns, collaborate with non-profit organizations, or launch their own initiatives to aid in animal welfare efforts. This could involve anything from funding veterinary treatment for pets in low-income households to providing resources for shelters struggling to meet their animals' needs.

Fundamentally, being a pet influencer isn't merely about entertaining followers with cute or funny pet antics. Many pet influencers utilize their platform's power to advocate for change, raise awareness about important issues, and inspire their audience to take action. Their influence extends beyond their follower count, reaching into the realm of social good, proving that pet influencer fame can be about much more than just likes and shares.

3. Community: The journey of having a famous pet can lead to a unique and rewarding outcome beyond fame or monetary benefits - it can assist you in creating a thriving, supportive community of individuals who share your passion for pets.

A pet influencer often becomes the focal point around which a community of fellow pet enthusiasts congregates. These communities are formed on the basis of a shared interest, a mutual love for pets, which transcends geographical boundaries and cultural differences. They bring together individuals from diverse walks of life who find a common ground in their affection for animals.

This community can offer tremendous support to pet owners. Whether it's advice on pet care, tips on training, or recommendations for the best pet products, the collective wisdom and experiences of the community members can serve as a valuable resource. Moreover, during challenging times, like dealing with a pet's illness or behavioral issues, the community can provide emotional support and understanding that might be hard to find elsewhere.

Friendship is another beautiful aspect of these communities. Bonds formed over shared interests can evolve into meaningful friendships. People connect, interact, and in many cases, form friendships that extend beyond the digital sphere. Pet meet-ups, events, and conventions provide opportunities for these online friends to meet in person, further strengthening the bonds within the community.

Sharing the joy that pets bring is another essential function of these communities. From sharing photos and videos of pets' cute antics to celebrating pets' birthdays and milestones, the community becomes a platform for spreading happiness and positivity. It's a space where each pet's unique personality can be celebrated and cherished.

In this light, the fame of a pet influencer offers the potential to create a sense of togetherness and camaraderie. The community that forms around a pet influencer is not just a group of followers but rather, a network of like-minded individuals who draw support, friendship, and shared joy from their collective love for pets. Thus, a pet's fame can serve as a catalyst, bringing people together and creating a vibrant, engaging, and supportive community that extends far beyond simple pet ownership.

4. Creativity and Personal Growth: The endeavor of steering a successful pet influencer account is one that demands not only the exhibition of creativity but also an astute sense of marketing. These requirements, however, are not just challenges, but opportunities for self-expression, learning, and personal development. This journey can indeed be a gratifying personal adventure that fosters an environment of continuous growth and learning.

The world of pet influencers is a vibrant and competitive space, one that necessitates a distinctive voice and aesthetic. A unique part of this journey is the opportunity to express creativity, from devising original themes for posts, storytelling through captions, to creating engaging video content. The task of regularly producing unique, engaging content requires constant brainstorming and pushes the boundaries of one's creative skills. It offers an exciting platform to express oneself and showcase the unique personality of the pet.

Simultaneously, managing a pet influencer account offers a wealth of experience in marketing and brand management. It is a journey that involves understanding audience demographics, optimizing posts for maximum engagement, and developing promotional strategies for various social media platforms. Furthermore, it requires learning how to negotiate and maintain profitable partnerships with brands, which equates to gaining hands-on experience in business dealings and contracts.

Strategic thinking and decision-making are other skills that are honed on this journey. Every move, from pivoting content strategy based on audience feedback, to choosing the right brand partnerships, requires a tactical approach. This fosters an understanding of business strategy and planning, an invaluable skill set in many professional fields.

Running a pet influencer account also necessitates resilience and adaptability. The road to success may come with criticism and challenges such as fluctuations in follower count or engagement rates. Learning to handle these gracefully contributes to personal growth, cultivating a sense of resilience and a knack for problem-solving.

Lastly, the journey also offers a unique opportunity for self-discovery and expression. It's a platform that allows sharing of personal stories, experiences, and the exploration of one's creative passions. It can lead to the discovery of new interests and skills, as well as the satisfaction of turning a love for pets into a shared experience with a like-minded community.

The process of managing a successful pet influencer account goes beyond merely achieving online fame for your pet. It's a rewarding personal journey that encourages continual learning, self-expression, and growth. It offers a challenging yet fulfilling path that can lead to acquiring new skills, personal development, and a deeper understanding of digital marketing dynamics.

Setting Realistic Expectations and Goals

While the idea of turning your pet into an Instagram star may seem exciting, it's essential to approach this journey with realistic expectations and clearly defined goals. Remember, every pet influencer who has achieved fame has a unique story. What worked for one may not work for another.

Firstly, understand that achieving high levels of success as an Instagram pet influencer often takes time and consistent effort. The Internet is saturated with adorable pet content, so standing out from the crowd requires creativity, persistence, and a lot of patience.

Secondly, while financial gain is a possibility, it should not be your primary motivator. If you're getting into pet influencing purely for the money, you may find yourself disappointed. The initial monetary returns are typically modest, and only a small percentage of pet influencers reach the levels of income that can replace a full-time job.

Thirdly, it's crucial to consider the wellbeing of your pet. While some pets enjoy the attention and stimulation of being photographed and filmed, others may find it stressful. It's crucial to ensure that your pet's comfort and happiness are always the top priority.

In the next chapter, we will discuss how to determine if your pet is suited to be an Instagram star and how to start your journey.

Remember, the goal is not to force your pet into something unnatural but to share the joy that they bring into your life with the world. If approached with the right intentions and understanding, turning your pet into an Instagram star can be a fun and rewarding experience.

CHAPTER TWO

Defining Your Pet's Unique Personality and Brand

Identifying Your Pet's Special Traits and Quirks

Every pet is a unique entity, possessing a distinct blend of traits and idiosyncrasies that differentiate them from the rest of the animal kingdom. Recognizing these unique characteristics and projecting them to the world forms the essence of your pet's online persona, laying the ground-work for their digital identity.

Perhaps you have a bunny that has an unusual penchant for bananas, or a dog whose relentless pursuit of his own tail never fails to induce bouts of dizziness. It could be that your cat bucks the trend by showing an uncommon love for water, or your bird has an uncanny ability to mimic the sounds of your home appliances. These quirks and unusual habits serve a dual purpose - they amuse and captivate your followers, while simultaneously portraying your pet as a relatable and genuine character.

The process begins with an inventory of your pet's characteristics, behaviors, and daily routines. Reflect on your pet's personality: Are they the energetic, playful type, or do they prefer to laze around? Do they exude an adventurous spirit or are they more of a homebody? Is your pet mischievous or do they exude a calm demeanor? Any specific habits or behaviors, like a dog burying his toys in the backyard, a cat's love for laser pointers, or a bird's fascination with mirrors, should also be noted.

Beyond behavior, physical characteristics also play a significant role in crafting your pet's online identity. Your pet's physical traits, whether it's a unique coat pattern, a distinctively shaped tail, unusual size, a pair of expressive eyes, or a distinctive shape of ears, can be defining features that set your pet apart from others.

Don't forget to consider your pet's favorite activities, their most loved toys, and their interactions with other animals and humans. The relationships your pet forms can be a charming aspect of their online persona, adding depth to their story. Perhaps your pet has a close bond with a neighborhood animal, or they've formed an unlikely friendship with another species. Or maybe your pet has a special bond with a member of the family. These elements bring an added layer of interest and intrigue, making your pet's story all the more compelling.

Remember, the goal is to paint a holistic picture of your pet that resonates with your audience. The more your followers relate to your pet and their antics, the more invested they become in your pet's story. The process of identifying and highlighting your pet's special traits and quirks is the bedrock upon which you can build an engaging, authentic, and endearing online persona for your pet.

Creating a Consistent Theme and Style for Your Pet's Instagram Account

Just as every influential brand thrives on the power of its unique visual identity, so should your pet's Instagram account. This concept stretches beyond the confines of individual posts and extends to encapsulate the general ambiance and 'feel' of your pet's digital footprint.

Initiate this process by contemplating your pet's 'aesthetic'. This may be determined by numerous factors, such as the environment in which you live, the decor style of your home, or simply your personal aesthetic preferences. Your chosen aesthetic might be vibrant and filled with color, or it could be sleek and modern, with minimalist tones. Perhaps you lean towards a rustic and natural look, exuding a cozy, down-to-earth vibe. The choices are limitless, and the best part is that they can be anything that suits your pet's personality and your creative vision.

Next, delve into the composition of your photos. Would you opt for close-up shots that emphasize your pet's unique expressions and details? Or maybe you're inclined towards wider shots that capture the context of your pet's environment, thus telling a broader story? Perhaps you prefer candid shots that depict your pet in the midst of their everyday life, capturing spontaneous moments of joy, curiosity, or relaxation. Or maybe you're drawn to more elaborate, themed photoshoots that add an element of drama and creativity to your pet's narrative. The format of your content is another aspect to consider. Will your feed predominantly feature still images, or will it include videos that bring your pet's antics to life? Or perhaps a balanced mix of both would best depict your pet's lively personality?

An integral part of curating your pet's consistent visual style is the use of filters and editing techniques. Your selection of filters can significantly impact the mood of your photos, whether it's a warm, sun-kissed filter that evokes a sense of nostalgia, or a vibrant, high-contrast filter that makes the colors pop. Your editing style can add a layer of cohesion to your feed, tying your posts together and making them instantly recognizable to your followers.

Consistency, after all, is the linchpin of building a recognizable and cohesive brand for your pet. By maintaining a consistent theme, style, and aesthetic, you're not just creating a visually appealing Instagram feed, but also laying the foundation for your pet's unique brand identity. This consistency lends familiarity to your pet's online presence, strengthening your audience's connection with your pet and fostering a sense of loyalty and anticipation for your future posts.

Developing a Strong, Memorable Pet Brand

Developing a Strong, Memorable Pet Brand: Having pinpointed your pet's unique traits and outlined a vision for your Instagram aesthetic, the next step is the synthesis of these elements into a compelling, unforgettable brand.

The brand you construct for your pet is not merely an amalgamation of their visual aesthetics or individual traits. It encompasses the emotions and sentiments that your pet's account incites in its followers. Does it provoke laughter and amusement? Does it inspire joy or offer a much-needed dose of cuteness and relaxation? Recognizing and capitalizing on these emotional themes can offer a valuable guide for your content creation process.

The process of creating a robust brand also necessitates consistency in the tone and style of your captions, as well as your interactions with followers. If you've chosen to communicate in your pet's voice, ensure to maintain this voice consistent across all posts. This voice could be mischievous, philosophical, goofy, or diva-like - the crucial part is that it should remain uniform across your content, solidifying your pet's online persona.

To add another dimension to your brand, consider creating a unique hashtag specific to your pet's account. Not only does this serve to augment your brand, but it also amplifies the discoverability of your content. Additionally, it furnishes your followers with a fun, interactive way to engage with your brand and share content relating to your pet.

Developing a robust, memorable brand for your pet is indeed a creative endeavor, one that involves a blend of experimentation, receptive feedback from your audience, and an openness to adapt and evolve. When executed successfully, it sets your pet apart from the multitude, crafting a unique and endearing online persona that followers can't resist revisiting.

In the subsequent chapters of this guide, we'll delve deeper into these branding fundamentals and demonstrate how to implement them effectively. We will guide you through tactics for growing your follower base and engaging efficiently with your audience. Regardless of whether you're taking your initial steps into the pet influencer world or are a seasoned pet-fluencer looking to optimize your approach, there will be valuable insights for everyone as we journey further into the world of pet influencers.

CHAPTER THREE

Capturing Paw-some Photos and Videos

Creating compelling, high-quality content is a vital aspect of your pet's Instagram success. Great photos and videos will not only help define your pet's brand but also engage your followers and attract new ones. In this chapter, we delve into some practical tips for capturing and editing paw-some content.

Basic Photography and Videography Tips for Pet Photoshoots

1. Patience is Key: It's essential to bear in mind that you're collaborating with an animal who lacks the human concept of what a photoshoot entails. Your pet won't inherently understand the need for a perfect pose or a steady gaze at the camera. This necessitates patience on your part, and it's absolutely crucial that you ensure the entire process is enjoyable for your pet.

Understandably, working with pets can pose unique challenges. Unlike human models, animals don't respond to verbal instructions in the same way, and their attention spans can be unpredictable. It's common for pets to become distracted, restless, or even nervous when confronted with unfamiliar situations, such as the bright lights, props, or costumes often used in photoshoots. As their handler, it's your responsibility to ensure your pet's well-being, comfort, and enjoyment throughout the process.

To encourage cooperation, incorporate plenty of playtime and rewards into your photoshoots. Use your pet's favorite toys or treats to catch their attention, and ensure there are plenty of breaks for rest and play. Positive reinforcement will make your pet more inclined to participate in future photoshoots, turning what could be a stressful experience into a fun, enjoyable game.

Always remember that your pet's comfort and happiness should be the top priority. Never force your pet to participate in a photoshoot if they are uncomfortable or showing signs of stress. The goal is to create enjoyable content that showcases your pet's personality and uniqueness, and this can only be achieved when your pet is happy and relaxed.

Ultimately, cultivating patience and maintaining an emphasis on fun can turn the process into an enjoyable bonding experience for you and your pet, rather than a chore. With patience and understanding, you can successfully navigate the unique challenges of pet photography, creating beautiful and authentic content that truly captures the spirit of your pet.

2. Capture their Personality: The most captivating photos and videos are invariably the ones that seize your pet's authentic personality in the frame. They distill the essence of your pet's individuality, portraying a snapshot of their character that resonates with your audience. These may be dynamic action shots, like a dog poised mid-air to catch a frisbee, showcasing their agility and playfulness, or a

cat stealthily stalking a toy, capturing their innate hunter instinct. These vivid depictions serve as exciting glimpses into your pet's energetic and playful side, allowing your followers to engage with their active moments.

Alternatively, they could be tranquil and serene images, like your pet luxuriously napping in their favored spot, perhaps curled in a sunlit corner or nestled against a cozy blanket. Such images offer a contrast to the high-energy shots, presenting the calm, relaxed side of your pet's personality. They resonate with followers by showcasing the endearing everyday moments of your pet's life, evoking feelings of peace and contentment that are universally relatable.

Remember that it's not always about the grand gestures or perfect poses. Often, the most compelling content is derived from the simple, candid moments where your pet's individuality shines through. Perhaps it's the contented purr of your cat as they bask in a patch of warm sunlight, the curious tilt of your dog's head when they hear a new sound, or the amusing antics of your bird as they play with their favorite toy. It's in these unscripted moments that the heart of your pet's personality is truly revealed.

Capturing your pet's personality extends beyond just visual content. Incorporating narratives or anecdotes about your pet into your captions can further help your audience connect with your pet's unique character. For example, sharing a funny story about your pet's latest mischief or reflecting on their endearing habits can enrich your content, providing context and depth that elevate a simple photo or video into a vibrant snapshot of your pet's life.

Ultimately, the art of capturing your pet's personality lies in paying attention to their unique quirks and behaviors, understanding their likes and dislikes, and patiently waiting for the perfect moment to immortalize them in a photo or video. In doing so, you create a deeper connection between your pet and their audience, fostering a sense of familiarity and affection that will keep your followers eagerly anticipating your next post.

3. Use Treats and Toys: To facilitate the process of capturing your pet's most engaging moments, it can be immensely helpful to have your pet's preferred toys or treats readily available. These items can serve as effective tools to command their attention and elicit photogenic actions or expressions.

Pets, much like people, exhibit heightened engagement and emotion when interacting with items they are fond of. A favorite squeaky toy or a cherished treat can ignite a spark of excitement, joy, or focus in your pet, resulting in genuine and captivating expressions. These instances, when your pet's attention is fully absorbed by their favorite object, often yield the most authentic and engaging content.

Using toys can stimulate action shots that illustrate your pet's playful, energetic side. For instance, a frisbee toss can lead to a dynamic mid-air catch shot for a dog, or a feather wand can capture a cat's agile pounce. These snapshots, full of movement and vitality, are likely to create engaging and memorable content for your audience.

On the other hand, treats can be used to reward desired behaviors or to hold your pet's attention for more static or posed shots. The promise of a tasty treat can encourage your pet to hold a pose, look in a certain direction, or display specific expressions, offering you more control over the composition of your shots.

However, while treats and toys can be powerful tools in your pet photography toolbox, they should be used judiciously. Overuse can lead to distraction or even over-stimulation for your pet, potentially leading to stress or health issues, especially with regards to excessive treat consumption. The focus should always remain on making the experience enjoyable for your pet, with their health and well-being as the top priority.

When employed mindfully, treats and toys can be a game-changer in pet photography, helping you to capture a range of authentic, heartwarming, and entertaining images that truly reflect your pet's unique personality and charm.

4. Experiment with Perspectives: One aspect that can significantly elevate your pet photography is experimenting with a variety of perspectives. Shooting solely from your standing height may not fully capture the essence of your pet or offer the diversity that keeps your pet's feed engaging and fresh.

To truly capture your pet's world, consider getting down to their eye level. This perspective can offer a more intimate look into your pet's life, granting your audience a glimpse of the world from their viewpoint. Such shots can reveal details that are often overlooked from a human height, such as the texture of your pet's fur, the concentration in their eyes, or their playful interactions with their environment.

Aerial or bird's-eye view shots can add another layer of interest to your pet's feed. Looking down at your pet from above can create unique, often charming compositions that reveal patterns and contexts missed at ground level. Whether it's your cat curled up into a perfect circle, your dog lounging on a rug that complements their fur, or your bird's eye-catching plumage displayed against a contrasting background, aerial shots offer an expansive view of your pet's world.

Close-ups can also offer a uniquely engaging perspective. Focusing on your pet's face, paws, tail, or other distinct features can create a sense of intimacy and allow your followers to appreciate the smaller details that make your pet special. Such shots can capture the sparkle in your pet's eyes, the whimsical tilt of their ears, or the intricate patterns of their fur, providing a fresh, focused perspective of your pet's individuality.

Additionally, don't forget to experiment with different angles, such as shooting from below or incorporating diagonal lines, to add dynamism and intrigue to your photographs. Play with the placement of your pet within the frame, following the rule of thirds for balanced compositions or deliberately breaking it for creative effect.

Remember, variety is the spice of life, and this applies to your pet's feed as well. By regularly varying your perspective and shooting angles, you can keep your content diverse and engaging, maintaining your audience's interest and enticing them to come back for more of your pet's captivating world.

5. Plan Your Photoshoots: While spontaneous captures can sometimes serendipitously yield magical, candid moments that charm your audience, there is a significant value in taking a more structured approach to your pet photography. Planning your photoshoots in advance can provide you with a greater level of control over various elements of your imagery, ensuring you can consistently produce high-quality content that aligns with your pet's brand.

Begin with scouting an appropriate location for your shoot. This could be within your home, where your pet feels most comfortable, or it could be an outdoor location, such as a nearby park or beach, for a change of scenery.

When selecting a location, consider the backdrop it will provide and how it complements your pet's personality and the theme of your shoot. A serene garden might work well for a tranquil cat, while a bustling park could be perfect for showcasing an energetic dog.

The time of day is another crucial aspect to consider. If shooting outdoors, leverage the 'golden hours' — the first hour after sunrise and the last hour before sunset. During these periods, the lighting is soft, warm, and diffused, which can yield beautiful, ethereal shots. If shooting indoors, find a time when natural light illuminates your chosen location optimally. The right lighting can enhance the mood, emphasize your pet's best features, and avoid unflattering shadows or harsh, overexposed areas.

Prop selection is another key part of the planning process. From toys and treats to costumes and furniture, props can add visual interest, evoke emotions, and inspire actions or reactions from your pet. Ensure any props you choose are safe for your pet to interact with and match the overall aesthetic and theme of your shoot.

Think about the shots you want to capture in advance. Envision the composition, the angles, the perspective, and your pet's actions or expressions. Of course, it's essential to remain flexible, as pets often have their own ideas about how a photoshoot should go! However, having a clear plan in mind will give you a solid starting point and help you respond creatively to any unplanned moments.

Ultimately, planning your photoshoots allows you to align your content more cohesively with your overall branding, and ensures that every photo or video you share is purposeful and impactful. The aim is to create a thoughtful narrative with your pet as the star, ensuring each post on your pet's feed contributes to a compelling, engaging story that resonates with your audience.

6. Use Burst Mode for Action Shots: Pets are naturally dynamic, filled with energy and vitality that often result in animated, sometimes unpredictable, movements. If your pet is particularly active or playful, capturing their movements in a single, perfect shot can be challenging. This is where the burst mode on your camera becomes an invaluable tool in your pet photography arsenal.

Burst mode, also known as continuous shooting mode, allows you to take several photos in rapid succession by simply holding down the shutter button. This is especially useful for photographing pets in motion, as it greatly increases the odds of capturing that one perfect frame amidst their flurry of activity.

Whether it's your dog bounding after a thrown ball, your cat in mid-leap, or your bird spreading its wings to take flight, burst mode can freeze these split-second actions into a series of still images. This can yield stunning action shots that portray your pet's energy, agility, and grace, which may not be evident in more static photos.

Once the photoshoot is over, you can sift through the series of images at your own pace. You might find that one particular frame captures your pet's movement at its peak, with every detail sharply in focus. Alternatively, you might find a sequence of frames collectively tells a compelling story of your pet's action. Remember, the 'perfect' shot isn't necessarily the most technically flawless one; it's the one that most effectively communicates the joy, determination, or elegance of your pet's movement.

It's also worth noting that while burst mode can be a game-changer for action shots, it does require ample storage space, as it quickly generates a large number of high-resolution images. Make sure to regularly back up and clear your storage to continue capturing your pet's dynamic moments without interruption.

In summary, leveraging the burst mode on your camera can open up a whole new dimension in your pet photography, allowing you to capture your pet's lively spirit and movements in a captivating, immersive way that engages and delights your audience.

7. Focus on the Eyes: The eyes are said to be the windows to the soul, a sentiment that holds as true for animals as it does for humans. Pets often communicate their emotions, intentions, and individuality through their eyes, which can be remarkably expressive. By choosing to focus on your pet's eyes in your photos, you can create a powerful, emotional connection between your pet and your audience, drawing viewers into the image and offering them a deeper insight into your pet's unique personality.

Whether your pet's eyes are glistening with mischief, reflecting a serene calm, or beaming with unbridled joy, capturing these moments can make your photos particularly engaging. Close-ups or portraits where your pet's eyes take center stage can be especially impactful. They can reveal subtleties like the unique color and pattern of their iris, the reflection of their surroundings, or the contrasting textures of their fur and eyes, which all contribute to a more compelling image.

To focus on your pet's eyes, you may need to experiment with your camera's focus settings. Use a large aperture (small f-number) to create a shallow depth of field, blurring out the background while keeping your pet's eyes sharp and in focus. This can help to draw attention to the eyes and reduce potential distractions in the photo.

Proper lighting is also crucial for capturing the eyes beautifully. Natural, diffused light can often be the most flattering, illuminating the eyes without causing harsh shadows or reflections. Catchlights, or the reflection of a light source in your pet's eyes, can add life and sparkle to your image. Try to position your pet so that light falls into their eyes, creating catchlights that add depth and dimension.

However, remember that your pet's comfort should always come first. Never force them to stare directly at a bright light or use flash photography, which can harm their eyes.

Focusing on your pet's eyes in your photography can breathe life into your images, create a powerful emotional resonance, and convey a sense of your pet's individuality. With practice and patience, you can master the art of capturing your pet's expressive eyes, producing images that resonate with your audience and tell a deeper story of your pet's character and experiences.

8. Create a Relaxing Environment: To capture your pet's most natural and authentic moments, it's essential that they feel at ease during the photoshoot. When your pet is relaxed and comfortable, they're more likely to provide natural poses and expressions that reflect their genuine personality, leading to more compelling and engaging content for your audience.

Begin by choosing a familiar and comfortable location for your photoshoot. This could be your pet's favorite lounging spot in your home, a well-trodden path in the local park, or any place where your pet typically feels safe and at ease. Familiarity breeds comfort, so holding your photoshoot in a place your pet knows well can help to minimize their stress or nervousness.

Keep the atmosphere calm and pleasant during the shoot. Avoid loud noises or sudden movements that could startle or stress your pet. If you're photographing indoors, you might play soft, soothing music, or if you're outdoors, you might select a quiet, secluded spot.

The energy and mood of the people present can also significantly impact your pet's comfort. If you're tense or impatient, your pet will likely pick up on these emotions and react accordingly. Try to maintain a relaxed, patient, and positive attitude throughout the shoot, offering your pet plenty of praise and affection.

Make the photoshoot a fun experience for your pet by incorporating playtime and treats. This can help keep your pet interested and engaged, and it can also provide opportunities for capturing joyful and dynamic moments. However, never force your pet to pose in a way that they find uncomfortable or distressing. Prioritizing your pet's wellbeing over getting the 'perfect' shot is not only ethical but also leads to more authentic and engaging content.

Lastly, remember that pets, like humans, can have off days too. If your pet seems uninterested or agitated, it's best to postpone the photoshoot for another time when they're feeling more up to it.

By creating a relaxing environment for your photoshoot, you're setting the stage for authentic, high-quality content that reflects your pet's true personality, fostering a deeper connection with your audience. This approach emphasizes respect and consideration for your pet's comfort and wellbeing, reinforcing the bond between you and your pet and leading to more enjoyable and successful photoshoots in the future.

Using Natural Lighting and Capturing Your Pet's Best Angles

Lighting is a crucial element of photography, and natural light is generally the most flattering. Whenever possible, photograph your pet near a window or outdoors. However, avoid direct sunlight, which can cause harsh shadows and overexposed shots. Overcast days or shady spots provide the best natural light.

Golden Hours: Photographers swear by the "golden hours" - the hour after sunrise and the hour before sunset. During these periods, the sun's position low on the horizon creates a soft, warm, and diffused light that bathes the world in a golden glow. This distinctive lighting condition can produce stunning, atmospheric shots that add a magical touch to your pet photography.

The golden hours provide a uniquely flattering light that can enhance the aesthetic appeal of your photos. The warm tones can illuminate your pet's fur or feathers, highlighting their texture and color in a way that midday sunlight often fails to capture. The low angle of the sun creates long, soft shadows that add depth and dimension to your images, giving them a more three-dimensional feel.

Furthermore, the golden hours often coincide with periods of increased activity for many animals. This could be an opportune time to capture your pet during their most active or playful moments, adding a dynamic element to your photos.

However, utilizing the golden hours requires some planning. You'll need to check the sunrise and sunset times for your location and plan your photoshoot accordingly. Also, keep in mind that the duration and quality of the golden light can change based on the season, weather, and geographical location.

Moreover, while the golden light is indeed beautiful, it can also present challenges. The low light conditions may require you to adjust your camera settings, such as using a larger aperture, slower shutter speed, or higher ISO. You may also need to experiment with different angles and positions to capture the best light and avoid unwanted shadows or silhouettes.

Shooting during the golden hours can infuse your pet photography with a magical, ethereal quality that sets your images apart. With practice and patience, you can leverage this enchanting light to produce stunning, atmospheric photos that showcase your pet in a unique and captivating way.

Beware of Mixed Lighting: Navigating the realm of lighting in photography can be tricky, especially when it comes to mixing different types of light. One of the common pitfalls to be aware of is the mixing of artificial light with natural light, as this can create confusing and often unflattering colors and shadows in your photos.

Artificial lights, like those in your home, often have a different color temperature compared to natural sunlight. For example, incandescent lights can produce a warm, yellowish glow, while fluorescent lights may give off a cooler, bluish light. When combined with natural daylight, which is generally more neutral, these different light sources can create a mismatch in colors in your photos, leading to unnatural-looking scenes.

This color mismatch is due to what is called "white balance". Each type of light source has a different white balance, and your camera tries to adjust for this to make white objects appear truly white, but when there are multiple light sources with different color temperatures, the camera can struggle to accurately balance the colors.

Moreover, mixing artificial light with natural light can lead to complex shadow patterns. Each light source will cast its own shadow, and when combined, they can create a layered effect that can distort the sense of depth and texture in your photos. These overlapping shadows can distract from the main subject - in this case, your pet - and detract from the overall visual harmony of the image.

So, how do you deal with mixed lighting? If possible, try to control your light sources. If you're indoors, turn off artificial lights and use only natural light from windows. Conversely, if you're shooting at night or in a dark room, rely solely on artificial lights to avoid the introduction of mixed colors and shadows.

If you can't avoid mixed lighting, you might need to correct the colors in post-processing. Many photo editing software like Adobe Lightroom or Photoshop offer tools to adjust the white balance and reduce color casts.

While it's possible to create interesting and creative effects with mixed lighting, it's generally safer to stick with one type of light source at a time, especially if you're just starting out with pet photography. This can help you maintain control over the color balance and shadows in your photos, resulting in more natural and harmonious images.

Angles for Different Pets: The choice of camera angle can significantly influence the perception and emotional impact of your pet photographs. Different pets, due to their varied sizes, shapes, and behaviors, might require different angles to fully capture their unique characteristics.

For smaller pets, such as hamsters, guinea pigs, or small dog breeds, shooting from their level or even from a lower perspective can work wonders. This approach can help accentuate their petite size and make them appear larger than life. By getting down on their level, you also immerse the viewer in the pet's world, making the image feel more personal and intimate.

On the other hand, for larger pets like big dog breeds or horses, a variety of angles can highlight different features and expressions. You could shoot from above to underscore their size and strength, or you might want to try an eye-level shot to capture their personality more directly. Shooting from below can offer a unique and interesting perspective that showcases their grandeur.

Birds, reptiles, and other exotic pets also come with their own unique set of considerations when it comes to angles. For birds, capturing them in flight or perched high above can emphasize their freedom and elegance. For reptiles, close-ups that highlight their textured skin or expressive eyes can make for intriguing shots.

Beyond size and species considerations, remember that each pet, just like humans, will have their "good side." Spend time observing your pet and figuring out which angles flatter them the most. Do they look particularly adorable when they tilt their head a certain way? Does their fur catch the light just right when they're lounging in their favorite spot? Perhaps they have a signature pose or a distinctive feature that can be accentuated from a particular angle.

These considerations are part of the fun and challenge of pet photography. It's a constant process of learning and discovery, a journey guided by observation and experimentation. As you spend more time with your pet, you'll start to see their individual quirks and nuances that can be used to create captivating and unique images.

So, go ahead, experiment with various angles, observe your pet's unique qualities, and keep in mind that the most impactful photographs are often those that capture the true essence and personality of your pet. Every photoshoot will provide new insights, helping you continually refine your skills and deepen your understanding of your pet's character.

Editing Techniques to Enhance Your Pet's Visual Content

Even the best photos can usually benefit from a bit of editing. There are numerous photo-editing apps available that can enhance your pet's photos and videos.

1. Crop and Composition: In photography, sometimes it's the little things that make a big difference. Take cropping, for example. A minor adjustment to the crop of a photo can substantially change its impact and appeal. Cropping allows you to eliminate distracting elements, bring attention to the subject, or change the orientation of the photo. A crucial rule of thumb to keep in mind when cropping is the 'rule of thirds.' This guideline divides the image into nine equal parts using two equally spaced horizontal lines and two equally spaced vertical lines. The idea is to place your pet or the most important elements of your image along these lines or at their intersections to achieve a more balanced, dynamic composition. This can be far more visually interesting than just centering your subject.

2. Brightness, Contrast, and Saturation: Even the most seasoned photographers occasionally need to make adjustments to their photos post-shoot, and that's where basic editing tools come in. Brightness can adjust the overall lightness or darkness of the image. Contrast alters the difference between the darks and lights in the photo. Saturation controls the intensity of colors. These simple yet powerful tools can dramatically improve a photo's lighting and make the colors more vibrant or muted depending on your

desired effect. However, a word of caution: don't overdo these adjustments. The goal is to enhance the photo's natural beauty, not make it look overly edited or artificial.

3. Filters: Filters are pre-set editing effects that can quickly and easily add a certain mood or style to your photos. They can help establish a consistent aesthetic on your pet's Instagram feed, tying your posts together with a common visual theme. If you choose to use filters, try to stick with the same one or two across your posts. This helps maintain a consistent look and feel and makes your feed more recognizable to your followers. However, like all editing tools, filters should be used judiciously. A heavily filtered photo can sometimes look unnatural or inauthentic.

4. Retouching Tools: Retouching tools offer a level of fine-tuning that can perfect an image. They can be used to remove unwanted objects or blemishes from the background, fix small imperfections, or even enhance specific features. Perhaps there's an unsightly trash bin in the background of an otherwise perfect shot of your pet, or maybe a strand of hair fell into your pet's eye just as you took the photo. Retouching tools allow you to clean up these little distractions, keeping the focus on your pet.

Remember, editing should enhance the storytelling in your photograph, not overshadow it. The best edits are often the ones that aren't immediately noticeable—they subtly enhance the photo without drawing attention to themselves. Always strive for balance when editing, keeping the attention on your pet's unique charm and personality.

While it's important to create visually appealing photos and videos, the essence of your pet's Instagram account is your pet. Make sure your content showcases their personality, character, and the joy they bring into your life. In our next chapter, we will delve deeper into growing your pet's Instagram presence and ensuring it is not just visually appealing but also engaging, entertaining, and true to your pet's unique charm.

CHAPTER FOUR

Writing Engaging Captions and Stories

Your captions and stories are where your pet's character really comes to life. These are the spaces where you share the charming anecdotes, the endearing quirks, and the heartwarming moments that make your pet truly special. In this extended chapter, we'll explore the art of crafting engaging captions and utilizing Instagram Stories in depth.

Crafting Captions That Tell a Story and Engage Your Audience

A good caption can be the difference between a quick double-tap and a new, engaged follower. Here's how to craft the perfect pet caption:

1. Use Your Pet's Voice: Humanizing your pet and giving them a distinct voice of their own can be an incredibly effective strategy for engaging with your followers. Imagine, for a moment, what your pet might say if they could talk. What would their personality be like? Would they be mischievous and cheeky, wise and philosophical, or bubbly and enthusiastic? Perhaps they would have a distinct sense of humor, or maybe they'd possess a dramatic flair.

This technique involves writing captions and interacting with your followers from your pet's point of view. Suddenly, it's not just a picture of a cat lounging in the sun, it's a hilarious monologue about the struggles of choosing the perfect spot for a nap. It's not merely a photo of a dog playing fetch, but an epic tale of a heroic quest for the elusive tennis ball.

Using your pet's 'voice' can make your posts more engaging, fun, and relatable. It gives depth to your pet's personality and creates an immediate and charming character that followers can fall in love with. Your audience isn't just following a pet's account; they're following the adventures, thoughts, and antics of a full-fledged character.

This approach can also give you a unique way to talk about the products or services you might be promoting. Instead of a straightforward advertisement, it becomes a story – an experience that your followers can enjoy, laugh at, and share.

Remember, consistency is key. Once you've established a voice for your pet, stick with it. This will help solidify your pet's character and make your account a go-to place for entertaining and charming content.

Of course, this approach requires a level of creativity and a willingness to play and experiment. It might take some time to find the perfect 'voice' for your pet. But when done right, it can set your pet influencer account apart and create a strong emotional bond between your pet and your followers, which is absolutely invaluable in the world of social media.

2. Tell a Story: Every picture is worth a thousand words, and those words can be powerfully used to weave an engaging narrative around your pet's antics. A caption that

tells a story, instead of merely describing what's happening in the photo, can be a powerful tool to captivate your audience. By painting a vivid picture with your words, you can pull your followers into the world of your pet, making them laugh, smile, or even tear up.

Perhaps it's the hilarious chronicle of your cat's latest 'hunting' adventure, going after a harmless piece of string as if it were a fierce jungle predator. Maybe it's the endearing tale of how your dog insists on bringing you your slippers every evening, even if they occasionally bring the wrong pair. Or perhaps it's the heartwarming narrative of how your pet bird seemed to sense you were having a tough day and kept you company with their cheerful chirping.

This storytelling approach can help your followers feel like they're part of your pet's life. They become invested in your pet's daily adventures and mishaps, eagerly waiting for the next 'chapter' in your pet's life. They start seeing your pet as a character with an ongoing narrative, rather than just an animal posing for cute photos.

Don't be afraid to get personal. If your dog comforted you after a difficult day, share that. If your cat did something silly that made you laugh when you were feeling down, let your followers know. Sharing these authentic moments can create a strong emotional connection with your followers, making them more engaged and invested in your pet's life.

However, it's crucial to keep the balance right. While it's great to share your pet's life story, remember that the primary focus should always be on your pet. Use your storytelling to enhance your pet's charm and appeal, and not to overshadow it.

So, the next time you're about to post a photo of your pet, take a moment to think about the story behind it. By turning a simple caption into a captivating tale, you can engage your audience on a deeper level, making your pet's Instagram account a source of joy and entertainment for your followers.

3. Ask Questions: One way to boost the level of interaction on your pet's Instagram account and foster a sense of community among your followers is by asking questions in your captions. This simple yet effective strategy can significantly increase the number of comments on your posts and enhance the sense of connection your followers feel towards your pet.

These questions can be as simple as asking, "What are your pets up to today?" or "Does anyone else's dog love to chase their tail as much as mine does?" Alternatively, you can use this as an opportunity to learn more from your audience, with questions like, "Can anyone recommend durable toys for a super playful kitten?" or "What's your favorite dog-friendly hiking trail?"

Additionally, you can ask for opinions, such as "Should we get a new bandana in blue or red?" or create fun interactive opportunities like, "Caption this photo of my pet doing something funny." The goal is to encourage your followers to engage and interact with your posts, to not only increase your reach and visibility but also build a sense of community.

These interactions can be beneficial in multiple ways. First, they boost your engagement rates, which can increase your account's visibility due to the way Instagram's algorithm works. Secondly, by reading and responding to the comments, you can gain valuable insights into your followers' preferences, which can guide your future content creation. Lastly, these conversations help to foster a sense of community among your followers. They don't just follow your pet's account; they're part of your pet's life.

Remember, social media is not just about broadcasting; it's about fostering dialogue and building relationships. By asking questions and encouraging conversation, you're not just growing your pet's Instagram account; you're creating a vibrant, interactive community of pet lovers who share a bond with your pet. This sense of connection can be incredibly rewarding, both for you and your followers.

4. Include Calls to Action: One of the keys to driving deeper engagement and interaction on your pet's Instagram account is through the use of compelling calls to action (CTAs) in your captions. A call to action is an instruction to the audience designed to provoke an immediate response, usually using an imperative verb such as "like," "share," "tag," or "click."

These CTAs serve to guide your audience towards a specific action, be it to amplify your post's reach, drive traffic to a particular webpage, or simply generate more interaction on your post. For instance, you could ask your followers to "like and share this post if you think my cat's antics are hilarious," or to "tag a friend who needs a smile today."

If you have a new blog post, YouTube video, or merchandise on your pet's website, you could ask your followers to "click the link in our bio to check it out." When hosting a giveaway or contest, you can instruct your followers to "enter by tagging two friends who would love to win."

By including CTAs, you make it clear what action you'd like your followers to take, thereby increasing the likelihood of them doing so. But remember, while CTAs can be very effective, they need to be used judiciously. Make sure they align naturally with your content and don't come across as too promotional or demanding.

Also, ensure to vary your CTAs to prevent your posts from becoming repetitive or predictable. Keep them relevant and engaging, matching the tone and style of your pet's brand. When done right, CTAs can be a powerful tool in boosting engagement, driving traffic, and building a more active and involved community around your pet's Instagram account.

Expanding on Utilizing Instagram Stories to Showcase Your Pet's Daily Life

Instagram Stories are a vital tool for any pet influencer. Here's how to make the most of them:

1. Share Your Pet's Routine: Consistently posting about your pet's daily life can significantly deepen the connection your followers feel towards your pet. By providing regular updates on your pet's routine, from their meals to their playtime and naps, you keep them present in your followers' minds and establish a consistent content stream. It's like sharing snippets from a day in your pet's life, which can feel more personal and allow your audience to relate more easily to your pet.

2. Utilize 'Day in the Life' Stories: One engaging way to leverage Instagram features is through 'Day in the Life' stories, where you document your pet's daily activities in real-time. This can include everything from your pet's morning stretches and breakfast routine to their outdoor explorations, play sessions, and evening cuddles. Sharing such authentic, unfiltered moments from your pet's day can create a strong sense of intimacy, making your followers feel as if they're a part of your pet's life.

3. Leverage Instagram's Interactive Features: Instagram's interactive features such as the question sticker and polls

can be incredibly useful for boosting engagement. Use the question sticker to solicit pet-related advice or to run a fun Q&A about your pet. Alternatively, use the poll feature to involve your followers in decision-making processes like choosing your pet's next toy or deciding on a costume for Halloween. Such activities not only encourage follower participation but also provide valuable insights into your audience's preferences.

4. Show Behind-The-Scenes Content: In addition to showcasing your pet's best moments, it can be beneficial to reveal what happens behind the scenes. This might involve sharing the comedic chaos of staging a pet photoshoot, the adorable mess your pet makes during mealtime, or the hilarious aftermath of a mischievous spree. Such content can be surprisingly entertaining and relatable, demonstrating that the reality of pet ownership isn't always picture-perfect. This approach adds an extra layer of authenticity to your pet's brand and makes your account more relatable, further strengthening the bond between your pet and their online community.

5. Run Themed Days or Series: Introducing themed days or content series can bring a sense of anticipation and

structure to your pet's feed. This might be something like 'Mischief Mondays' where you share your pet's latest naughty antics, 'Throwback Thursdays' featuring cute photos or stories from your pet's earlier days, or a weekly series where you explore different pet care topics. Such themes not only make your content more varied and engaging but also give your followers something to look forward to.

Deep Dive into Balancing Humor, Heart, and Authenticity in Your Content

Each Instagram post is an opportunity to connect with your audience. Here's how to strike the right balance:

1. Humor: A key ingredient to the success of many pet influencers is humor. Pets are naturally amusing and their antics can provide much-needed lightness and laughter. Whether it's your dog's futile attempts to catch their tail, your cat's seemingly dramatic reactions to the smallest changes, or your bird's humorous mimicking of household sounds, these comical moments can captivate your followers and attract more engagement. Keep your eyes open for funny, unexpected moments and share them with your audience - they will appreciate the laugh.

2. Heart: An essential aspect of a successful pet influencer account is the heartfelt connection between you and your pet. Sharing tender moments of companionship, affection, and care can strike a chord with your followers. These moments remind your audience of the unique bond they share with their own pets, triggering emotions and making your content more impactful. Whether it's a picture of your pet cuddling up with you, a story about how your pet comforted you during a difficult time, or a post appreciating your pet, such content can foster a sense of warmth and relatability in your pet's online persona.

3. Authenticity: Authenticity is the cornerstone of a successful pet influencer account. Followers appreciate and relate more to accounts that present the genuine experience of pet ownership, which isn't always glamourous or perfect. Share your pet's bad hair days, the occasional mischief they get into, their quirky dislikes, as well as their adorable, picture-perfect moments. This honesty makes your pet's account more relatable, helps to establish trust with your audience, and enhances the appeal of your pet's brand. Remember, your followers are here to experience the joy and reality of your pet's life, not a picture-perfect fantasy. It's the authenticity that keeps them coming back.

The world of pet influencers is one of joy and fun, but it's also one of connection and community. With every photo, video, caption, and story, you're not just building your pet's brand; you're also building a community of people who love your pet as much as you do. That's a powerful thing. Use it well, and your pet's Instagram account can be a source of joy for thousands, even millions, of people around the world.

CHAPTER FIVE

Growing Your Pet's Instagram Following

Turning your pet into an Instagram star isn't just about creating great content - you also need to attract and retain a loyal following. In this chapter, we'll explore proven strategies for growing your pet's Instagram following.

Tips for Attracting and Retaining Followers

Growing your following is about more than just getting people to click the 'Follow' button. You want followers who are genuinely interested in your pet and will engage with your content. Here are some strategies to achieve that:

1. Engage with Your Followers: An active interaction with your followers is critical to building a strong, engaged community. Respond to comments on your posts, engage in their content by liking and commenting, and consider even following back some of your active followers. You can also host Q&A sessions in your stories or go live on Instagram to interact with your followers in real-time. These actions can make your followers feel valued and acknowledged, which will enhance their loyalty and engagement with your pet's content.

2. Run Contests or Giveaways: Organizing contests or giveaways can be a powerful method to boost engagement and attract new followers. You can collaborate with pet-related brands for sponsored giveaways or host a photo contest where followers share their own pet photos using a specific hashtag. The promise of a reward can motivate your followers to actively participate, and the shared content can increase your account's visibility on the platform, attracting more potential followers.

3. Share User-Generated Content: Encouraging and sharing user-generated content can not only provide you with a consistent stream of content but also make your followers feel valued and included. You can encourage your followers to tag your account or use a unique hashtag when they share photos or videos of their pets. Once you get permission, repost this content on your feed or stories, and don't forget to give credit to the original poster. This strategy can foster a sense of community around your pet's account, increase engagement, and provide diverse content to your audience.

Consistency and Posting Frequency Best Practices

Consistency is key on Instagram. Followers should know what to expect from your pet's account in terms of both the type of content and how often it's posted. Here's how to achieve this:

1. Formulate a Detailed Posting Strategy: The first step towards maintaining an effective social media presence is to develop a detailed and robust posting strategy. This involves understanding and analyzing when your followers are most active and engaged. Use the gathered data to identify the prime times for posting content - these time slots

are when your posts are most likely to be seen and interacted with by your audience. It's recommended to stick to this calculated schedule as closely as possible to optimize your reach and engagement. Today's digital landscape provides numerous user-friendly tools and applications that can assist in scheduling your posts effectively and efficiently. By leveraging these, you can ensure your posts go live at the designated times, even if you are not online or available at that moment, maximizing your visibility and interactions.

2. Foster a Consistent and Unique Brand Aesthetic: The significance of maintaining a uniform aesthetic cannot be overstated when it comes to building and strengthening your pet's brand. This applies not only to your visual content but also to the text accompanying it - the captions. You could choose a specific filter, color palette, or a visual theme for your photographs to ensure that your posts are distinguishable and carry a consistent tone. Similarly, it's advantageous to adopt a unique writing style or tone for your captions - perhaps something that embodies your pet's personality or character. Consistency in your aesthetic, both visual and textual, allows your audience to instantly recognize your content in their feed, enhancing recall value and reinforcing your brand identity.

3. Strike a Perfect Balance Between Consistency and Over-posting: One of the crucial aspects of managing a successful social media presence is knowing how often to post. It's important to remain consistent and regular with your posts to ensure you stay on your followers' radar and keep them engaged. However, there is a fine line between being consistent and overloading your followers with content. It's best to steer clear of the latter as it could potentially lead to follower fatigue and decrease engagement rates. A generally accepted best practice is to aim for at least one post per day but try not to exceed three posts within a 24 hour period. By maintaining this balance, you can ensure that your content remains fresh and engaging for your followers without overwhelming them, thereby fostering a positive and interactive relationship with your audience.

Using Hashtags, Geotags, and Engagement Strategies to Boost Visibility

Utilizing Instagram's features can help increase your pet's visibility on the platform. Here's how:

1. Hashtags: Hashtags serve as powerful discovery tools on Instagram, often driving the way people come across new and interesting content. To effectively harness the power

of hashtags, employ a balanced mix of popular, generic hashtags such as #petsofinstagram along with more targeted, niche-specific ones that accurately portray your pet's unique characteristics or breed, like #tri-colorcorgi. This strategy enables your posts to reach a broader audience, while also tapping into specific communities that have a keen interest in content like yours.

2. Geotags: If you're at ease with sharing your geographical location, incorporating geotags into your posts can significantly amplify your local visibility. Geotags are especially beneficial for users residing in pet-friendly cities or neighborhoods as they can help draw attention from local followers or fellow pet enthusiasts in your vicinity. This method can cultivate a strong local community around your pet's brand and also provide opportunities for local collaborations or meet-ups.

3. Engagement Groups: Another effective tactic to escalate your pet's brand visibility is by joining pet-related engagement groups on Instagram. These are communities where members mutually agree to interact with - like and comment on - each other's posts, thereby augmenting their individual engagement metrics. Being part of such active

groups not only enhances your profile's visibility but also provides you access to a network of similar content creators, giving you an opportunity to learn, collaborate, and grow together. The cumulative effect of increased engagement often leads to improved visibility on followers' feeds and the Instagram Explore page, potentially boosting your follower count.

By following these strategies and best practices, you can steadily grow your pet's Instagram following. But remember, it's not just about the numbers. Your goal should be to cultivate an engaged, interactive following that truly appreciates your pet's unique charm and personality.

CHAPTER SIX

Networking and Collaborating with Other Pet Influencers

Networking and collaboration are powerful strategies to boost your pet's Instagram presence. By aligning with other pet influencers, you can tap into their audience and increase your pet's visibility. In this chapter, we'll guide you on how to identify potential collaboration partners, engage with them, and take part in pet-themed challenges and events.

Identifying Potential Collaboration Partners

Successful collaborations start with finding the right partners. Here are some tips for identifying potential collaborators:

1. Similar Size: When exploring potential collaborations, it's highly beneficial to identify other pet-themed accounts that boast a similar follower count to your own. The reason for this is twofold. First, they are likely to appreciate and recognize the value that such a partnership could bring, as you can both provide a similar level of exposure and cross-promotion. Second, collaborations with accounts that mirror your own in terms of size and influence often result in more balanced and mutually beneficial outcomes.

By connecting and forming alliances with these similar-sized accounts, you can mutually expand your respective audience bases. Your content will be exposed to their followers and vice versa, resulting in a win-win situation where both parties can enjoy increased engagement and follower growth. Furthermore, such collaborations can lead to the formation of valuable connections within your niche community, which can provide learning opportunities, inspire fresh content ideas, and open up avenues for future partnerships.

So, don't hesitate to reach out to these accounts with collaboration proposals. Remember, the essence of social media is being 'social'. Building relationships, engaging with other similar accounts, and even sparking friendly conversations can significantly enhance your pet's online presence and overall brand.

2. Similar Niche: When planning collaborations or simply looking to expand your network, it's vital to consider accounts that concentrate on the same niche as your own. For instance, if you're managing a page dedicated to a rare breed of dog, align yourself with other accounts that spotlight the same breed. The advantage here lies in the shared interest and specialized knowledge both you and your potential partners can offer, thus, creating highly engaging and relevant content for your shared audience.

On a similar note, if your pet has a distinctive skill, characteristic, or feature - say, they're adept at skateboarding or perhaps they're uniquely identifiable with one eye - seek out other accounts that underscore these peculiar traits. The rationale behind this is that audiences following such specific traits or skills are likely to be deeply engaged and more interested in similar content, leading to higher engagement rates.

By aligning with similar niches, you can ensure that your collaborations are not only relevant to your followers but also increase the likelihood of captivating a larger audience that is genuinely interested in the specific content you produce. This strategy helps foster a sense of community among followers, enriches your content, and enhances your credibility within your specific niche.

3. Compatible Aesthetic and Values: An often overlooked yet crucial aspect of forging collaborations is the importance of partnering with accounts that echo a similar aesthetic and value system as your own. This harmonious alignment ensures that your shared content seamlessly blends with your existing posts, thus maintaining a consistent visual and thematic flow for your followers.

For instance, if your pet's brand is characterized by bright, vibrant images coupled with cheerful and positive captions, collaborating with an account that shares a similar sunny aesthetic and upbeat messaging will resonate better with your followers. Similarly, if your content focuses on promoting responsible pet ownership and adoption, a partnership with an account that also champions these values will reinforce your message and brand ethos.

The alignment of aesthetics and values doesn't just maintain consistency, it also reaffirms your brand identity and strengthens your relationship with your followers. By choosing collaboration partners whose content complements your pet's brand and image, you ensure that the shared content is authentic, relatable, and engaging to your audience, thereby enhancing your overall brand resonance.

Engaging with Other Pet Influencers on Instagram

Once you've identified potential collaborators, it's time to engage with them. Here's how to do it:

1. Practice Authentic Engagement: Engagement goes beyond simply liking posts; it's about fostering a genuine connection and actively participating in their online community. Regularly interact with their content by leaving thoughtful and meaningful comments, reacting to their stories, or even sharing their posts on your own story. This kind of authentic engagement not only shows apprecia-

tion for their work but also gives them a sense of your active involvement and interest in their content.

2. Initiate Direct Outreach: After you've established a presence in their online community, consider reaching out to them via a direct message. When expressing your interest in collaborating, maintain a polite and professional tone. Be clear and specific about your proposition - describe what kind of collaboration you have in mind, how it can be mutually beneficial, and why you believe your brands are a good fit. This approach shows your seriousness about the collaboration, making them more likely to consider your proposal.

3. Cultivate Lasting Relationships: It's important to remember that networking on social platforms like Instagram is not just about initiating one-off collaborations. It's about building enduring relationships. Keep the connection alive even after the collaboration has ended. Continue engaging with their content, support their initiatives, and be there to celebrate their milestones. This ongoing support is instrumental in fostering a strong network that values mutual growth, which can open up opportunities for more collaborations in the future.

Participating in Pet-Themed Challenges and Events

Taking part in challenges and events can also increase your pet's visibility. Here are some strategies:

1. Join Trending Challenges: Jumping on the bandwagon of trending challenges, such as the #BottleCapChallenge or #WhatTheFluff, is an excellent strategy to enhance your visibility on Instagram. These social media challenges often go viral, attracting a substantial amount of attention and engagement from users across the platform.

Participating in these challenges presents a fantastic opportunity to showcase your pet's personality and skills while engaging with a larger audience. It also allows you to produce fresh and engaging content that resonates with current trends, thereby maintaining relevance and capturing your followers' interest. Remember to use the associated hashtags effectively when posting your take on the challenge. This increases your chances of being discovered by users following the challenge, thereby significantly boosting your visibility.

Additionally, participating in such challenges demonstrates your active presence and involvement in the Instagram community. It shows that you are tuned into the latest happenings, keeping your content vibrant, engaging, and up-to-date. This can lead to increased engagement rates, more followers, and a more dynamic online presence for your pet's brand.

2. Attend Pet-Themed Events: Attending pet-centric events, whether they're local gatherings, conventions, or Instagram live sessions hosted by renowned pet influencers, can serve as a valuable avenue for networking and expanding your follower base. These events often attract like-minded individuals and pet enthusiasts who are likely to take an interest in your pet's brand.

By actively participating in these events, you get a chance to showcase your pet's unique qualities and personality, thereby piquing the interest of potential new followers. Additionally, it allows you to meet and interact with other pet owners and influencers in your niche, opening up opportunities for future collaborations and partnerships.

You can also share your experiences at these events through your Instagram posts and stories. Sharing behind-the-scenes content or highlights of the event not only keeps your existing followers engaged but also showcases your active participation in the community. This active involvement strengthens your brand image, potentially leading to increased visibility, greater engagement, and a broader follower base.

3. Host Your Own Challenges or Events: Once you've garnered a significant following and established a firm footing in your niche, it's worth considering the organization of your own Instagram challenges or live events. This initiative can serve as a strong engagement magnet and reinforce your pet's standing as a prominent influencer within their specific niche.

Hosting your own challenge, such as a photo contest or a unique pet trick challenge, encourages your followers to actively engage with your content and share it within their circles. This creates a ripple effect, drawing more eyes to your page and potentially growing your follower base.

Similarly, live events like Q&A sessions, behind-the-scenes tours, or interactive playdates can offer your followers a more intimate look into your pet's life, fostering a stronger connection with your audience. These events can also be leveraged to collaborate with other influencers, further boosting your reach and engagement.

By initiating your own events or challenges, you're not only enhancing your visibility and engagement on Instagram but also positioning your pet as a leading figure within their community, reinforcing your brand's authority and influence.

By taking advantage of networking and collaboration opportunities, you can expand your pet's reach, gain new followers, and even make some new furry friends along the way. It's all part of the fun and rewarding journey of being a pet influencer.

CHAPTER SEVEN

Monetizing Your Pet's Fame

Once your pet has established a sizeable and engaged following, it's possible to monetize their fame. In this chapter, we'll guide you through partnering with pet-related brands, understanding the dynamics of sponsored content and affiliate marketing, and exploring the possibility of selling pet-related merchandise and products.

Partnering with Pet-Related Brands and Businesses

Brand partnerships can be a lucrative source of income for popular pet influencers. Here's how to approach it:

1. Implement Detailed Research on Potential Partners: Before venturing into any collaborations, it's imperative to meticulously examine prospective pet-related brands. Ensure they align seamlessly with the persona and image of your pet's brand. For instance, if your pet represents a breed associated with opulence or luxury, collaborations with upscale pet accessory brands or gourmet pet food providers might be the perfect fit. This compatibility not only ensures a natural and organic partnership but also enhances the likelihood of its acceptance and success with your audience.

2. Compile a Comprehensive Media Kit: A well-curated media kit acts as your brand's calling card, showcasing all the essential information about your pet's brand. This includes everything from your pet's unique brand personality, audience demographics, and engagement rates, to your past collaborations and their success stories. By presenting this data in an organized and visually appealing format, potential partners can swiftly grasp the value and potential benefits that a collaboration with your brand can bring. A professionally put together media kit can help you stand out and present your brand in a compelling light.

3. Initiate Professional Outreach to Potential Brands: With your media kit prepared, you're now set to approach the potential partners you've identified. When reaching out, ensure to maintain a professional demeanor and make your proposition explicit. Clearly outline the type of collaboration you're proposing - it could be anything from a sponsored post, product endorsement, giveaway, or even a joint event. Detail how such a partnership could generate mutual benefits, possibly resulting in increased visibility and enhanced engagement for both parties. This proactive, detailed, and professional approach can significantly bolster your chances of cementing valuable partnerships and expanding your pet's brand reach.

Understanding Sponsored Content and Affiliate Marketing

Sponsored content and affiliate marketing are two popular ways to monetize an Instagram account. Here's what you need to know:

1. Sponsored Content: In a sponsored post scenario, a brand compensates you to promote or feature their product within your content. While it presents a fantastic opportunity for monetization, it's crucial to handle spon-

sored content with care to ensure it aligns with your pet's brand image and voice. Even when incorporating promotional material, the content should continue to reflect your pet's authenticity and unique personality.

Disclosing sponsored content is a key aspect of maintaining transparency with your audience. Always clearly indicate when a post is sponsored, typically by including tags such as #sponsored, #ad, or #partner. This disclosure not only adheres to advertising guidelines but also nurtures a relationship of trust with your followers. It's important they know when you're recommending a product because you genuinely like it versus when you're doing so as part of a paid promotion.

Remember, maintaining your pet's authenticity in sponsored content can have a positive impact on your audience's perception of the brand you're promoting. It can result in more genuine engagement and a successful partnership with the brand, thus paving the way for more sponsorship opportunities in the future.

2. Affiliate Marketing: Another viable route for monetizing your pet's Instagram presence is through affiliate marketing. In this model, you partner with a brand to promote

their products and in return, receive a commission for any sales made through your unique referral link or code. The more your followers use your link or code to make purchases, the higher your earnings.

Affiliate marketing can be a valuable source of passive income, particularly once your pet's Instagram account has amassed a large and dedicated following. Followers who trust and value your recommendations are more likely to purchase products you endorse, thus increasing your potential earnings from affiliate links.

It's essential, however, to only endorse products that you genuinely believe in and that align with your pet's brand image. Promoting products that your pet uses and loves will resonate more with your audience, make your recommendations more credible, and ultimately lead to a more successful affiliate marketing strategy. As always, it's important to disclose your affiliate relationships to maintain transparency with your followers.

Selling Pet-Related Merchandise and Products

As your pet's fame grows, you might consider creating and selling your own products. Here's how:

1. Identify What Your Followers Want: One of the key success factors in creating and selling your own products is understanding what your followers want. Leverage your knowledge of your audience's interests, needs, and behaviors to devise product ideas that they would be excited about.

For instance, if your followers frequently comment on the adorable photos of your pet, a calendar featuring your pet's best photos could be a hit. If they admire your pet's accessories, launching a line of custom pet tags or pet accessories might garner considerable interest.

You could also directly ask your followers what they'd like to see. Polls or questionnaires can be an effective way to gather this insight. Instagram provides features such as "polls" or "questions" stickers in Stories, which you can utilize to solicit feedback and gauge interest in potential product ideas.

Once you have a good grasp of what your followers might be interested in, you can proceed with creating products that not only reflect your pet's brand but are also highly desirable to your audience. This strategy can significantly enhance the success of your merchandise and foster a deeper connection with your followers.

2. Find a Production and Delivery Partner: To streamline the production, sales, and shipping processes for your pet's merchandise, consider teaming up with established online platforms like Teespring or Shopify. These platforms offer comprehensive solutions for creating and selling custom products, making it easier for you to turn your product ideas into reality.

These platforms typically provide a user-friendly interface that allows you to design and customize your products, such as calendars, pet tags, or pet accessories, with ease. You can upload your pet's photos, logo, or designs to create unique merchandise that aligns perfectly with your pet's brand image.

Moreover, these platforms handle the entire sales and shipping process, eliminating the need for you to manage inventory or worry about order fulfillment. When someone purchases a product from your online store on these platforms, they take care of printing, packaging, and shipping the merchandise directly to your customers.

Utilizing these online platforms allows you to focus on promoting your products and engaging with your audience while leaving the technical aspects of production and order processing to the experts. This partnership simplifies the process of running an e-commerce store and empowers you to generate passive income from your pet's brand.

3. Promote Your Products: Your pet's Instagram account serves as the perfect platform to promote your newly created merchandise. Leverage your pet's popularity and engaging content to showcase the products you've designed.

Feature your products in high-quality photos with your pet as a model. Share captivating images of your pet using or wearing the merchandise, highlighting its appeal and relevance to your pet's brand image. Engaging visuals can entice your followers and create interest in your products.

Complement the visuals with compelling captions that describe the uniqueness and benefits of your merchandise. Share the story behind the creation of each product or why it holds significance to your pet's brand. Personal anecdotes or testimonials can add authenticity and strengthen your followers' emotional connection with the products.

To incentivize your followers to make purchases, consider offering special discounts or limited-time offers. Exclusive discounts can create a sense of urgency and encourage immediate action from your followers. You can use Instagram's features like countdown stickers or promotional posts to promote these limited offers.

Moreover, make use of Instagram Stories and highlights to provide behind-the-scenes glimpses of the product creation process, unveil new product launches, or feature customer testimonials and unboxing experiences. These stories can create excitement and curiosity around your products, motivating followers to explore and purchase them.

Remember to maintain authenticity and transparency throughout your promotional efforts. Your followers have grown to love your pet's content because of its genuine appeal, so ensure that your promotional posts still reflect that same authenticity.

Monetizing your pet's Instagram fame can be a rewarding experience. It can even become a full-time job, but always remember why you started. Continue prioritizing the joy and love that your pet brings to you and your followers.

After all, that's what truly makes your pet an Instagram star.

CHAPTER EIGHT

Maintaining Your Pet's Well-being and Privacy

While your pet's Instagram fame can be exciting and even profitable, it's crucial to always prioritize their well-being and privacy. In this final chapter, we'll explore ways to ensure your pet's happiness during photoshoots and events, setting necessary boundaries, and balancing their fame with their regular life.

Ensuring Your Pet's Happiness and Health During Photoshoots and Events

Creating content should never come at the expense of your pet's comfort and health. Here's how you can ensure their well-being:

1. Emphasize Safety and Comfort: The well-being of your pet should always be your top priority. Before engaging in any Instagram activities, ensure that your pet is comfortable and happy with what you're asking them to do. Whether it's wearing a costume, performing a trick, or being in a new environment, monitor their body language and behavior closely. If you notice any signs of stress, fear, or discomfort, stop immediately and find alternative ways to showcase their personality without causing distress.

2. Health Check-ups and Monitoring: Regular visits to the veterinarian are essential to ensure your pet's health and well-being. Engaging in Instagram activities may sometimes put additional stress on your pet's body or mind, so it's crucial to keep an eye out for any signs of stress-related health issues. Monitor changes in eating habits, behavior, or physical condition, and seek professional advice if you notice any concerns. Your pet's health should always come

first, and it's essential to strike a balance between your pet's Instagram presence and their overall wellness.

3. Manage Time and Energy: Pets, just like humans, have their limits when it comes to attention, energy, and patience. Keep photoshoots, trick sessions, or event appearances short and focused. Overextending these activities can lead to exhaustion and stress for your pet. Aim for quality over quantity - capture the best moments efficiently, and then allow your pet to rest and relax. It's essential to create a positive experience for your pet during their Instagram activities to maintain their enthusiasm and enjoyment over time.

Remember, your pet's Instagram presence should enhance their life, not detract from it. By prioritizing comfort, health, and appropriate time management, you can ensure that your pet's Instagram journey is a positive and enriching experience for both them and your audience.

Setting Boundaries and Protecting Your Pet's Privacy

Just like humans, pets need privacy and downtime. Here's how you can protect your pet's privacy:

1. Set Boundaries for Privacy: Remember that your pet's Instagram presence is just a curated glimpse into their life. You have the right to keep certain aspects of their life private. It's important to assess what you feel comfortable sharing and establish boundaries accordingly. Share content that reflects your pet's personality and brand without compromising their privacy or well-being.

2. Safeguard Your Pet's Safety: Be mindful of sharing specific locations that could potentially compromise your pet's safety. Avoid geotagging your home, frequent dog parks, or any location that might make your pet susceptible to unwanted attention or harm. Prioritize their safety and consider any potential risks associated with sharing location-related information.

3. Protect Your Pet's Image: Be selective about who you grant permission to use your pet's image and ensure it aligns with your pet's brand and image. When collaborating with brands, carefully evaluate the products or services being promoted to ensure they are in line with your pet's values and lifestyle. Ensure that any collaborations or endorsements are authentic and resonate with your audi-

ence, maintaining the trust they have placed in your pet's brand.

By respecting your pet's privacy, prioritizing their safety, and carefully managing their image, you can create a positive and responsible online presence for your pet. Balancing authenticity with caution will help ensure a positive and sustainable Instagram journey for your beloved companion.

Balancing Your Pet's Instagram Fame with Their Daily Life

Your pet is more than just an Instagram star. Here's how you can ensure a healthy balance:

1. Preserve a Regular Routine: Amid the excitement of managing your pet's Instagram presence, it's essential to maintain their regular daily routine separate from their online activities. Keep their meals, walks, and playtime consistent and structured, providing them with a sense of stability and familiarity. The regular routine serves as an anchor, ensuring that your pet's physical and emotional needs are met, regardless of their Instagram fame.

2. Unplug for Quality Bonding Time: While Instagram can be an enjoyable platform to showcase your pet's adventures and talents, it's crucial to dedicate unplugged bonding time to nurture your connection with them beyond the camera lens. Engage in activities that strengthen your bond, such as cuddling, interactive play sessions, or simply spending time in nature together. This intimate, technology-free time reinforces the idea that your pet is more than just an online presence; they are a beloved companion and cherished family member.

3. Thoughtful Retirement Planning: It's important to recognize that Instagram fame may not last indefinitely, and thus, it's crucial to plan for your pet's life after they retire from the limelight. Create a comprehensive retirement plan that considers their well-being and happiness post-Instagram journey. This could involve gradually reducing their online presence and transitioning to a quieter life away from the spotlight. Additionally, exploring new activities or hobbies that bring joy and fulfillment to your pet during their retirement ensures they continue to lead a meaningful life beyond their Instagram fame.

4. Nurturing Their Identity Beyond Instagram: While your pet's online presence may garner a substantial following, it's vital to remind yourself and your audience that they are multi-dimensional beings with diverse interests and emotions. Encourage your followers to appreciate your pet as more than just an Instagram star, showcasing their everyday moments, quirks, and genuine personality. Celebrate their unique qualities and remind your audience that Instagram is just one aspect of their well-rounded identity.

5. Create a Safe and Comfortable Environment: As your pet's Instagram presence grows, it's essential to ensure they always feel safe and comfortable during any photoshoots or public appearances. Pay close attention to their body language and stress levels, making necessary adjustments to the environment or situation if they seem overwhelmed. Prioritize your pet's well-being and be ready to step back or modify plans if they are not enjoying the experience.

By incorporating these practices into your pet's Instagram journey, you can create a balanced and enriching life for them both on and off the platform. Ultimately, your pet's happiness and well-being are at the core of their online presence, and nurturing a positive, authentic, and responsible experience ensures their overall quality of life remains exceptional.

Remember, your pet's well-being should always come first. Keep their happiness and health at the forefront of all your decisions as a pet influencer. Because at the end of the day, their wagging tail, contented purr, or cheerful chirp is the real reward of this journey.

CHAPTER NINE

Dealing with Challenges and Criticism

Every journey has its bumps, and being a pet influencer is no exception. In this chapter, we'll navigate through handling negative feedback, managing stress, avoiding burnout, and staying motivated even when setbacks occur.

Handling Negative Comments and Feedback

Not every comment will be a pat on the back. Here's how to handle negative feedback:

1. Maintain Professionalism: When facing negative comments, it's crucial to respond with professionalism and grace. Keep in mind that how you react reflects on your pet's brand and your own character. Avoid responding impulsively or defensively, as this can escalate the situation. Instead, take a moment to compose yourself and craft a thoughtful response. Address the concerns raised in a respectful manner, and show that you value feedback and are open to improvement.

2. Distinguish between Constructive Criticism and Trolling: Negative comments can come in different forms. Some may offer constructive criticism that can help you improve your content or approach. In such cases, it's essential to welcome the feedback and consider how you can implement positive changes. On the other hand, trolling comments are intended to provoke and create conflict. Learn to differentiate between the two and engage accordingly. Engaging with trolls is generally unproductive, so it's often best to ignore or gracefully disengage from such interactions.

3. Take a Break If Needed: Dealing with negative comments can be emotionally draining. It's perfectly okay to

take a break from reading comments if you find that they are affecting your mood or mental well-being. Stepping away from the negativity for a while can give you a chance to recharge and regain perspective. When you're feeling more resilient, you can return to address comments or concerns with a calmer mindset.

4. Seek Support: It's essential to have a support system to lean on when facing negativity online. Reach out to friends, family, or fellow pet influencers who can provide understanding, empathy, and advice. Talking to others who have experienced similar situations can help you navigate through challenging times and maintain a positive outlook.

5. Focus on the Positive: Negative comments can be disheartening, but remember that they are just a small fraction of your overall audience. Focus on the positive feedback and support you receive from your loyal followers. Celebrate the meaningful connections you've made and the joy your pet's content brings to others. A strong foundation of positive engagement can outweigh the impact of occasional negativity.

Handling negative comments and feedback is an inevitable part of being on social media. By responding professionally, differentiating between constructive criticism and trolling, taking breaks when needed, seeking support, and focusing on the positive, you can navigate through these challenges while maintaining your pet's brand authenticity and fostering a positive online community.

Managing Stress and Avoiding Burnout as a Pet Influencer

Being a pet influencer on social media can be a rewarding but demanding endeavor. Balancing your pet's Instagram presence with your personal life and well-being requires thoughtful planning and self-care. Here are some strategies to effectively manage your time and stress as a pet influencer:

1. Set a Schedule: To avoid feeling overwhelmed, establish a well-structured schedule that allocates specific times for photoshoots, content creation, and interacting with your followers. Plan ahead for themed posts or special events, allowing you to create content efficiently and maintain a consistent posting schedule. By setting dedicated time blocks for Instagram activities, you prevent it from taking

over every aspect of your life. Remember that quality over quantity matters, and it's okay to take breaks if needed.

Additionally, utilize time-saving tools like social media management platforms or scheduling apps to streamline your content posting process. This way, you can schedule posts in advance and have more flexibility to focus on other responsibilities.

2. Practice Self-Care: The demands of being a pet influencer can sometimes be all-consuming, but it's essential to prioritize self-care. Set aside time for relaxation, hobbies, exercise, or other activities that rejuvenate your mind and body. Remember that taking care of yourself is crucial to effectively care for your pet and manage their Instagram presence.

Incorporate mindfulness practices such as meditation or deep breathing to reduce stress and maintain mental clarity. Take regular breaks from screen time to prevent burnout and eye strain. Ensuring you have a healthy work-life balance will contribute to a more sustainable and fulfilling experience as a pet influencer.

3. Seek Support: Connect with other pet influencers who understand the unique challenges you face. Online pet influencer communities or social media groups can be a valuable resource for sharing experiences, seeking advice, and offering support. Having a network of like-minded individuals provides a sense of camaraderie and can help alleviate feelings of isolation or pressure.

Engage in constructive conversations with fellow influencers, exchange tips and strategies, and learn from each other's successes and setbacks. Remember that being a pet influencer is a journey, and having a supportive community can make the experience more enjoyable and enriching.

Being a pet influencer requires effective time management, self-care, and a supportive network. By setting a well-planned schedule, prioritizing self-care, and connecting with other influencers, you can manage the demands of your pet's Instagram presence while maintaining a healthy work-life balance and overall well-being.

Overcoming Setbacks and Staying Motivated

Being a pet influencer on Instagram can be a thrilling journey, but it's not without its challenges. During periods of slow growth or setbacks, it's essential to stay motivated and maintain a positive outlook. Here are some strategies to keep you inspired and focused on your pet's Instagram journey:

1. Keep the Big Picture in Mind: Remind yourself of the purpose and passion that led you to start your pet's Instagram account in the first place. Whether it's to spread joy, showcase your pet's unique qualities, promote responsible pet ownership, or simply share heartwarming moments with the world, hold onto this core vision. Reconnecting with your initial motivation during challenging times can provide renewed energy and keep you dedicated to your pet's brand and mission.

Whenever you face obstacles or feel discouraged, take a moment to reflect on the positive impact your pet's content has had on your audience. Read heartfelt comments or messages from followers who have been inspired or touched by your pet's Instagram presence. Focusing on the meaningful connections you've made can be a powerful source of motivation.

2. Celebrate Small Wins: In the dynamic world of Instagram, progress might not always be apparent at first

glance. However, every small achievement matters and is worth celebrating. Whether it's gaining a few new followers, reaching a milestone in engagement, or capturing a perfect shot of your pet, celebrate these moments of success.

Recognizing and appreciating the small wins can keep you motivated and positive, even during slower growth periods. Acknowledging these victories reinforces your efforts and reminds you that progress is still happening, albeit in smaller increments. Share these milestones with your followers, and they will likely celebrate alongside you, strengthening the bond between your pet's brand and your audience.

3. Adopt a Growth Mindset: Embrace challenges and setbacks as opportunities for learning and growth. Viewing them as part of the learning curve rather than failures can help you approach setbacks with resilience and determination. Understand that growth takes time, and success is often the result of perseverance and adaptability.

Embrace experimentation and continue to evolve your content and strategies based on what you learn. Take time to analyze your insights and audience feedback, and use this knowledge to make informed decisions. A growth mindset allows you to embrace the ups and downs of your pet's Instagram journey as stepping stones toward greater achievements.

Remember, the journey of being a pet influencer is as much about the process as it is about the outcomes. Staying motivated and positive, even during challenging times, will not only contribute to your pet's brand success but also enrich your personal growth and experience as a pet parent and content creator. By keeping the big picture in mind, celebrating small victories, and embracing a growth mindset, you'll be better equipped to navigate through any hurdles that come your way and continue to flourish as a pet influencer on Instagram.

Challenges and criticism are part of the journey to Instagram fame. By handling them with grace and resilience, you can ensure they make you and your pet stronger. Remember, this is a marathon, not a sprint. Keep going, and don't lose sight of the joy and love that your pet brings to your life and the lives of your followers.

CHAPTER TEN

Utilizing Other Social Media Platforms

While Instagram is a great starting point, expanding your pet's online presence to other platforms can yield even more opportunities. In this chapter, we'll delve into leveraging platforms like YouTube, TikTok, and Facebook for additional content and how to cross-promote your pet's content effectively across different channels.

Expanding Your Pet's Online Presence to Other Platforms

As your pet's Instagram presence grows, branching out to other social media platforms can open up exciting opportunities to reach new audiences and showcase your pet's unique personality in different ways. Here's a step-by-step guide to approaching this expansion:

1. Research the Platform: Each social media platform has its own set of features, audience demographics, and content styles. Before venturing into a new platform, conduct thorough research to understand its unique characteristics and user base. For example, TikTok may be more suitable for short and engaging videos, while Pinterest might cater to showcasing visually appealing photos and DIY ideas. By comprehending these differences, you can tailor your content effectively for each platform, optimizing its impact and appeal to the specific audience.

Additionally, examine the type of content that thrives on the platform you're considering. Explore how pet influencers or similar accounts operate there to glean insights and inspiration. Adapting your content strategy to suit the platform's environment is vital for success.

2. Start Slow: While the idea of expanding to multiple platforms might be tempting, it's best not to rush into it

all at once. Choose one or two platforms to begin with, and focus on building a strong presence there before expanding further. Starting slowly allows you to gain a deep understanding of the platform's dynamics, establish a loyal audience, and refine your content strategy to better suit the audience's preferences.

Remember that maintaining a consistent and engaging presence on each platform requires time and effort. By starting with a select few, you can dedicate the necessary attention to nurturing your pet's brand and audience relationships, ensuring a strong foundation for future growth.

3. Consistency is Key: As your pet expands to other platforms, consistency becomes crucial. Your pet's brand identity should remain consistent across all platforms, including the pet's name, logo, visual style, and messaging. Consistency fosters recognition and reinforces your pet's image in the minds of their fans, making them easily identifiable across various platforms.

While adapting content to suit each platform's format and audience is important, the core essence of your pet's brand should remain intact. This coherence creates a seamless experience for your followers and strengthens their emotional connection with your pet's unique persona.

Expanding to other social media platforms can be a valuable strategy for broadening your pet's reach and engaging with diverse audiences. By conducting thorough research, starting with a deliberate pace, and maintaining consistency, you can approach this expansion strategically and unlock new avenues for showcasing your pet's charm and appeal.

Leveraging YouTube, TikTok, and Facebook for Additional Content Opportunities

Expanding your pet's presence to various social media platforms provides exciting opportunities to showcase their personality and engage with diverse audiences. Tailoring your content to each platform's unique features can maximize its impact and appeal. Here's a closer look at the content opportunities on YouTube, TikTok, and Facebook:

1. YouTube: Longer Videos and Vlog-style Content

YouTube's platform is ideal for longer-form videos that allow you to delve deeper into your pet's adventures and showcase their unique skills. Consider creating vlog-style content that takes your audience along on your pet's daily activities or outings. This can include a day in the life of your pet, fun outings to pet-friendly locations, or behind-the-scenes glimpses of your pet's training sessions or photo shoots.

Moreover, YouTube provides an excellent platform for showcasing your pet's special tricks or skills in more extensive video formats. Creating tutorials or instructional videos on how you trained your pet can be both informative and entertaining for your viewers.

2. TikTok: Short, Entertaining Videos and Trending Challenges

TikTok thrives on short, snappy content that captures attention quickly. Embrace the platform's fun and fast-paced nature by creating engaging videos showcasing your pet's adorable moments, funny antics, or creative tricks. Consider jumping on trending challenges or using popular soundtracks to add a current and entertaining twist to your content.

Participating in dance routines, duets, or lip-syncing with your pet can also be a hit on TikTok. The platform's emphasis on quick and entertaining content offers an excellent opportunity to showcase your pet's charming personality in bite-sized pieces.

3. Facebook: Photos, Videos, Longer Text Updates, and Community Building

Facebook offers a versatile platform for sharing various types of content. Share eye-catching photos and engaging videos of your pet's adventures and special moments. Longer text updates can provide insights into your pet's life, training progress, or personal anecdotes that resonate with your audience.

Facebook Groups can be an effective way to create a community around your pet. Engage with followers through discussions, polls, and exclusive content for group members. Establishing a dedicated community fosters a stronger connection with your audience and encourages loyal followers to support your pet's journey.

Incorporating content opportunities unique to each platform can help you craft a well-rounded and compelling presence for your pet across social media. Remember to stay true to your pet's brand identity while leveraging the strengths of each platform to create content that resonates with their respective audiences.

Cross-Promoting Your Pet's Content Across Different Channels

Cross-promotion is a powerful strategy to ensure that your pet's audience on one social media platform knows about their presence on others. By strategically sharing content and utilizing platform tools, you can drive traffic between platforms and maximize your pet's exposure. Here's how to effectively implement cross-promotion:

1. Share Teasers: Create anticipation and curiosity among your followers by sharing teasers of your pet's content across different platforms. For example, post a short clip or snippet from a YouTube video on Instagram or Twitter, enticing your audience to watch the full video on YouTube. Similarly, share an engaging excerpt from a Tik-Tok video on Facebook, inviting your followers to view the complete video on TikTok. This approach not only piques interest but also encourages your followers to explore your

pet's presence on other platforms, expanding their engagement and reach.

2. Use Platform Tools: Social media platforms often offer built-in tools for seamless cross-promotion. For instance, Instagram allows you to share your posts directly to Facebook, reaching both audiences with a single click. Utilize these features to your advantage and share your pet's content across multiple platforms effortlessly. By tapping into these tools, you can amplify your pet's visibility and encourage followers to explore their presence across various platforms.

3. Include All Links: Ensure that your pet's social media profiles are interlinked. Include links to all their social media platforms in every bio, description box, and wherever applicable. For example, include links to your pet's YouTube channel, TikTok account, and other relevant social media profiles in their Instagram bio. This way, followers visiting any of your pet's profiles can easily navigate to other platforms and discover more content.

Additionally, consider adding a "Link in Bio" option in your Instagram posts to direct followers to your pet's latest video, blog post, or any other valuable content on a different platform. This simplifies the process for your audience, making it easier for them to access more of your pet's engaging content.

By implementing cross-promotion techniques, you can cultivate a cohesive and connected online presence for your pet. Strengthen your pet's brand across platforms, encourage followers to explore different content formats, and maximize their reach to new audiences, ultimately establishing a dynamic and engaged community of pet lovers.

Diversifying your pet's online presence can maximize their reach and open up new content possibilities. By understanding the unique features of each platform and cross-promoting effectively, you can ensure your pet's fame extends beyond Instagram. They'll be not just an Instagram star, but a bonafide internet sensation!

CHAPTER ELEVEN

Giving Back and Supporting Animal Welfare Causes

With fame comes responsibility, and your pet's Instagram success can be leveraged to make a significant impact. In this final chapter, we'll explore how you can use your pet's platform to raise awareness for important causes, partner with animal welfare organizations, and educate your followers on responsible pet ownership.

Using Your Pet's Fame to Raise Awareness for Important Issues

As your pet's popularity grows on social media, you have a unique opportunity to make a positive impact and advocate for causes you care about. Here's how to use your pet's platform to bring about change and make a difference:

1. Choose Causes You Care About: The first step in using your pet's influence for good is to identify causes that are close to your heart. Consider issues that are relevant to your pet's brand and align with their personality. Whether it's raising awareness about animal homelessness, promoting responsible pet ownership, supporting animal welfare organizations, or advocating for specific pet-related diseases, choosing a cause you are passionate about will give your advocacy authenticity and sincerity.

2. Spread Awareness: Utilize your pet's platform to educate and inform your followers about the causes you support. Create informative posts that highlight the importance of the issue, its impact on animals or the community, and ways people can get involved. Share resources, articles, and statistics to raise awareness and foster understanding among your audience.

Engage your followers in conversations related to the cause, encouraging them to share their thoughts and experiences. By sparking dialogue, you can build a community of compassionate individuals who care about the same issues and are willing to take action.

3. Lead by Example: As a pet influencer, your actions can be a powerful way to inspire and encourage your followers to take part in positive change. Show your audience how you're actively supporting the cause you care about. This could involve volunteering at a local animal shelter, participating in fundraising events, or adopting a rescue pet.

Sharing your personal experiences and involvement with the cause allows your followers to connect with you on a deeper level. It also demonstrates that your advocacy is not just limited to social media, but that you actively walk the talk in your everyday life.

Remember, using your pet's influence for positive change is not just about gaining likes or followers. It's about leveraging your platform to advocate for meaningful causes and create a real impact in the lives of animals and the pet community. By choosing causes you are passionate about, spreading awareness, and leading by example, you can make a difference and inspire others to join you in making the world a better place for pets and animals.

Partnering with Animal Welfare Organizations and Charities

Partnering with reputable organizations can significantly amplify your pet's advocacy efforts and make a more substantial impact on the causes you care about. Here's how to effectively collaborate with organizations to further your advocacy:

1. Research Potential Partners: Take the time to research and identify organizations that align closely with the cause you're advocating for. Look for reputable and established organizations that have a track record of making a positive difference in the area of interest. Ensure that their values align with yours and that they are transparent about their mission, goals, and use of funds. Engaging with organizations that share your passion and dedication will foster a more meaningful and productive partnership.

Reach out to the organizations and discuss your shared interests and potential collaboration opportunities. Be clear about your pet's brand identity and how it aligns with the organization's mission, as this will help them see the value of partnering with you.

2. Promote Their Work: Once you've established a partnership, use your pet's platform to promote the organization's work and initiatives. Share their campaigns, success stories, and achievements with your followers. Use your influence to raise awareness about the important work the organization is doing, helping to reach a broader audience and garner more support.

Highlight the impact of the organization's efforts through compelling storytelling and visuals, showcasing the lives they've positively affected. By shining a spotlight on their work, you not only promote their cause but also inspire your followers to get involved and support their mission.

3. Fundraise: Consider running fundraisers to support your chosen organization. You can directly appeal to your followers to donate to the cause or allocate a portion of the proceeds from your pet's merchandise sales to the organization. Fundraising initiatives can range from simple donation drives to more elaborate campaigns with specific goals and milestones.

Engage your audience in the fundraising process, keeping them updated on the progress and impact of their contributions. Transparency is key to building trust and encouraging continued support.

By partnering with organizations that share your passion and values, promoting their work, and fundraising on their behalf, you can leverage your pet's platform to create a greater positive impact on the causes you care about. Collaborating with established organizations adds credibility to your advocacy and demonstrates the power of collective efforts in making a meaningful difference in the lives of animals and the pet community.

Inspiring and Educating Your Followers on Responsible Pet Ownership

As a pet influencer, your platform can be a powerful educational tool to promote responsible pet ownership, advocate for animal welfare, and inform your audience about essential topics related to pets. Here's how to effectively use your pet's influence to educate your followers:

1. Share Responsible Practices: Use your platform to showcase responsible pet care practices. Regularly share

information about the importance of routine vet visits, vaccinations, and preventive healthcare measures. Offer guidance on proper nutrition and the significance of a balanced diet for your pet's overall well-being.

Additionally, educate your followers about the benefits of spaying and neutering pets, emphasizing the impact it can have on reducing pet overpopulation and improving their health. Encourage your audience to ask questions and seek advice from qualified professionals to ensure that they provide the best care for their own pets.

2. Promote Adoption: If your pet is a rescue or adopted, share their adoption story to inspire and encourage your followers to consider adopting their next pet. Highlight the joys and challenges of adoption, and discuss the rewarding experiences that come with providing a loving home to a pet in need.

Share success stories of other adopted pets to showcase the positive outcomes of adoption. Be open about the process of integrating an adopted pet into your family, as well as the patience and commitment required to address any challenges that may arise.

3. Discuss Important Topics: Utilize your platform to address crucial topics related to pets and animal welfare. Engage your audience in conversations about breed-specific legislation (BSL), the impact of puppy mills on animal health and welfare, and the consequences of selective breeding practices on certain breeds.

By providing well-researched information and evidence-based discussions, you can raise awareness about the importance of responsible pet breeding, ethical practices, and how legislation can impact the lives of animals. Encourage your followers to become advocates for positive change and to support initiatives that promote the welfare of animals.

Remember that education is an ongoing process, and your role as a pet influencer goes beyond sharing cute and entertaining content. By using your platform to promote responsible pet ownership, advocate for adoption, and discuss important animal-related topics, you can make a significant contribution to building a more informed and compassionate pet community. Empowering your followers with knowledge can lead to better-informed decisions and improved well-being for pets everywhere.

Your pet's Instagram fame gives you a unique opportunity to give back and make a difference. By raising awareness, partnering with organizations, and educating your followers, you can ensure your pet's fame has a lasting, positive impact beyond the adorable photos and entertaining videos. This is perhaps the most rewarding part of your journey as a pet influencer.

CHAPTER TWELVE

The Future of Your Pet's Instagram Stardom

As you establish your pet as an Instagram star, it's crucial to consider their long-term success and adapt to ever-changing social media landscapes. This chapter will delve into strategies for keeping up with social media trends and algorithms, exploring new content ideas, and planning for the long-term success of your pet's Instagram account.

Adapting to Changes in Social Media Trends and Algorithms

Social media platforms are constantly evolving, and as a pet influencer, staying up-to-date with these changes is essential to maintain relevance and maximize your impact. Here's how to effectively adapt to the ever-changing social media landscape:

1. Stay Informed: Make a habit of regularly reading articles, blogs, and official platform updates about the latest changes and trends in the social media world. Social media platforms often introduce new features, algorithm updates, and policy changes that can significantly impact your content's reach and engagement.

Being informed about these updates allows you to stay ahead of the curve and adjust your content strategies accordingly. Follow reputable industry experts, social media gurus, and official accounts of the platforms you use to stay informed about the latest trends and best practices.

2. Experiment: Embrace a spirit of experimentation and be open to trying new features or participating in viral trends. Social media platforms frequently introduce new features

that can enhance your content and engagement. For instance, you can explore Instagram's Reels, YouTube's Premiere feature, or TikTok's Duet and Stitch features to add diversity to your content and connect with your audience in innovative ways.

Participating in trending challenges or utilizing the latest filters and effects can keep your content fresh, engaging, and in tune with what's currently popular on the platform. By experimenting with new content formats, you can identify what resonates best with your audience and refine your strategy accordingly.

3. Analyze: Utilize the analytics tools provided by social media platforms, such as Instagram Insights, YouTube Analytics, and TikTok Pro, to gain valuable insights into your content's performance. Analyzing these metrics can help you understand how changes in the platform's algorithm or your content strategy impact your reach, engagement, and follower growth.

Pay attention to which types of content receive the most positive response, the peak times when your audience is most active, and the demographics of your followers. Use this data to tailor your content, posting schedule, and targeting to better align with your audience's preferences.

Remember that staying adaptable and flexible in your approach to social media is key to thriving as a pet influencer. Embrace continuous learning, be willing to experiment, and make data-driven decisions to optimize your content and grow your pet's presence on social media platforms. By staying informed, experimenting with new features, and analyzing performance metrics, you can navigate the evolving social media landscape and maintain a strong and impactful presence for your pet on various platforms.

Exploring New Content Ideas and Formats to Keep Your Audience Engaged

Sustaining engagement with your audience is vital for long-term success as a pet influencer. By actively involving your followers, diversifying your content, and staying true to your pet's unique brand, you can cultivate a loyal and dedicated audience. Here's how to keep your audience engaged:

1. Solicit Feedback: Actively seek input from your followers by asking them what they would like to see more of

on your pet's social media platforms. Use polls, surveys, or interactive story stickers to gather their preferences and opinions. By involving your audience in content decisions, you not only make them feel valued and connected but also gain valuable insights into what resonates with them.

Pay attention to comments and direct messages to understand your followers' interests, questions, and suggestions. Engaging in conversations with your audience shows that you are responsive and attentive to their needs.

2. Vary Content Types: To keep your feed engaging and exciting, diversify your content types. Balance between different formats such as photos, videos, stories, reels, and text posts. Each content type has its unique appeal and caters to different audience preferences.

Share candid moments, behind-the-scenes glimpses, educational posts, and entertaining videos to create a well-rounded and captivating experience for your followers. Experiment with new features and content ideas, while also highlighting your pet's strengths and charming personality.

3. Stay Authentic: While exploring new content types and trends, always stay authentic to your pet's brand and personality. Your followers are drawn to your pet because of their unique qualities, quirks, and charm. Maintaining authenticity builds trust with your audience and fosters a strong emotional connection.

Avoid compromising your pet's identity to fit in with viral trends or content that doesn't align with your pet's values. Let your pet's true character shine through, and embrace their genuine interactions with you and the world around them.

Audience engagement is a dynamic process that requires continuous efforts to understand your followers and deliver content that resonates with them. By seeking feedback, diversifying your content, and staying authentic, you can nurture a dedicated and enthusiastic audience that will continue to support your pet's journey as a beloved pet influencer.

Planning for the Long-Term Success and Legacy of Your Pet's Instagram Account

As a pet influencer, preparing for the future involves setting goals, preserving your pet's legacy, and considering the potential involvement of other pets in your Instagram strategy. Here's how to plan for the future to ensure a lasting impact:

1. Set Long-Term Goals: Establish clear, long-term goals for your pet's Instagram journey. Whether it's reaching a specific follower count, launching a product line featuring your pet's brand, or raising funds for a charity close to your heart, having defined objectives keeps you focused and motivated.

Breaking down these long-term goals into smaller, achievable milestones can make the journey more manageable and encourage you to celebrate the progress you make along the way.

2. Preserve Your Pet's Legacy: Recognize that one day, your beloved pet will cross the rainbow bridge. It's essential to think about how you'll handle this transition and preserve their legacy. Many pet owners choose to continue their pet's Instagram account as a tribute, sharing memories, photos, and stories to keep their spirit alive.

Alternatively, you might use the platform to advocate for causes your pet cared about or raise awareness about specific issues related to their breed or personality. Honoring your pet's legacy in a meaningful way can help you cope with the loss while maintaining the connection you've built with your audience.

3. Pass on the Baton: If you have other pets or plan to adopt more in the future, consider how they might fit into your Instagram strategy. Each pet has their unique qualities and charm, and they can play a significant role in continuing the legacy of their sibling star.

Introduce your audience to your new pet gradually, and be open about your journey of integrating them into your family. Celebrate the individuality of each pet and engage your audience in their growth and development. By involving your audience in your new pet's journey, you can continue to build a loyal and supportive community around your pet's brand.

Planning for the future as a pet influencer involves setting meaningful goals, honoring your pet's legacy, and embracing new opportunities that come with other furry companions. By staying true to your pet's brand, preserving their impact, and welcoming new additions to your Instagram journey, you can ensure that your pet's influence will leave a lasting and positive impression on the pet community and beyond.

As you build your pet's Instagram stardom, remember to keep an eye on the horizon. Adapting to changes, keeping your content fresh, and planning for the future will help ensure that your pet's star continues to shine brightly, bringing joy to you and your followers for many years to come.

CHAPTER THIRTEEN

Dealing with Media and Press Attention

As your pet garners more fame on Instagram, they are likely to attract attention from media and press. This chapter will guide you on how to navigate this new terrain, from preparing for interviews and media appearances to managing your pet's image and building relationships with journalists and bloggers.

Preparing for Interviews and Media Appearances

As your pet's fame grows, you may find yourself and your beloved companion invited to interviews and media appearances. Here's how to ensure you and your pet shine in the spotlight:

1. Anticipate Questions: Before the interview or appearance, take the time to anticipate potential questions that interviewers may ask about your pet, their journey to fame, and your role as a pet influencer. Consider questions about your pet's personality, any challenges or successes they've faced, and the inspiration behind their Instagram account.

Have thoughtful and concise responses ready, ensuring that your answers highlight your pet's unique qualities and the positive impact they've made on their audience. Being well-prepared will help you articulate your pet's story confidently and make the most of the opportunity to share their journey with a broader audience.

2. Rehearse: Practice makes perfect, and this applies to interviews as well. Rehearse your responses to the anticipated questions, either in front of a mirror or with a friend or family member. Practicing your answers will not only boost your confidence but also help you refine your delivery and ensure your messages come across clearly and concisely.

Pay attention to your body language and tone of voice during rehearsals. Presenting yourself with a friendly and approachable demeanor will enhance your pet's brand and make your interview more engaging and relatable.

3. Prepare Your Pet: If your pet will be included in the appearance, ensure they are comfortable with the environment and the people involved. Familiarize them with the location and the presence of cameras or lights, if possible. Bring their favorite treats or toys to keep them calm and relaxed during the appearance.

If your pet is comfortable with wearing costumes or accessories, consider incorporating these into the appearance to add a touch of fun and personality. However, always prioritize your pet's comfort and well-being, and avoid anything that might cause them stress or discomfort.

Media appearances are valuable opportunities to showcase your pet's brand and inspire others with their story. By preparing well, practicing your responses, and ensuring your pet's comfort, you can make the most of these appearances and leave a lasting positive impression on your audience and the broader public.

Managing Your Pet's Image in the Media

Media appearances can significantly influence how the public perceives your pet, so it's essential to carefully manage their image to stay true to their brand and maintain a positive reputation. Here's how to effectively manage your pet's image during media interactions:

1. Stay True to Your Pet's Brand: Just as you do on social media, ensure that the image portrayed in the media aligns with your pet's established brand and personality. Keep in mind the qualities and characteristics that make your pet unique and lovable, and convey these consistently in all media interactions.

Whether it's in interviews, photoshoots, or public events, stay authentic to your pet's natural behavior and charm. Avoid presenting your pet in ways that might contradict their true nature or make them uncomfortable.

2. Keep Control Over the Narrative: Before any media appearance, be clear about the message you want to convey about your pet. Plan key points you wish to highlight and stay focused on those during your interactions with the media.

Keep in mind the positive impact your pet has made through their platform, the causes they support, and the unique qualities that have garnered them a loyal following. Guide the conversation to align with your pet's mission and values, ensuring that the narrative reinforces their positive image.

3. Address Misconceptions: If you feel that your pet is being misunderstood or misrepresented during media appearances, don't hesitate to address and clarify any misconceptions. Politely and confidently correct any inaccuracies or misinterpretations about your pet or their story.

By actively participating in the narrative surrounding your pet, you can ensure that their image remains accurate and consistent with their actual personality and mission.

Remember, media appearances can be both exciting and challenging, so it's essential to approach them with careful planning and consideration. By staying true to your pet's brand, controlling the narrative, and addressing misconceptions when necessary, you can effectively manage your pet's image and continue to showcase them in the best possible light. This proactive approach will help maintain your pet's positive reputation and continue to build a strong and supportive community of followers and fans.

Building Relationships with Journalists and Bloggers

Having a network of media contacts can be invaluable for promoting your pet's growing fame and reaching a broader audience. Here's how to build and nurture meaningful relationships with media professionals:

1. Reach Out: Start by identifying journalists, bloggers, and influencers who cover pet-related stories or have an interest in animal-related content. Look for publications, websites, or social media accounts that align with your pet's brand and mission.

Once you've found potential contacts, reach out to them through email or direct messages. Introduce your pet and their story, highlighting their unique qualities and the impact they've made on their audience. Be concise, engaging, and considerate of their time, as media professionals receive numerous pitches regularly.

2. Offer Value: When reaching out to media contacts, provide them with exclusive stories or content about

your pet that they might find interesting and relevant for their readers or viewers. Share captivating anecdotes, behind-the-scenes glimpses, or exclusive updates that add value to their coverage.

Tailor your pitches to each media contact, showing that you've done your research and understand their audience and interests. Providing exclusive content will make your pet's story more appealing and increase the likelihood of them featuring your pet in their media outlets.

3. Stay Connected: Building and maintaining genuine relationships with media professionals is key to long-term success. Even when you don't have an immediate media need, stay in touch with your contacts. Share updates about your pet's latest achievements, milestones, or upcoming events.

Interact with their content, share their articles, and engage in conversations to show your support and interest in their work. Building a friendly and authentic connection will make them more inclined to consider featuring your pet in the future.

Building a media contact network takes time and effort, but it can significantly contribute to your pet's fame and impact. By reaching out, offering value, and staying connected with media professionals, you can secure valuable media coverage, expand your pet's reach, and further establish them as a beloved pet influencer in the online community.

Successfully handling media and press attention can amplify your pet's fame, helping them reach a wider audience. While it can be challenging, with preparation and strategy, you can ensure that your pet's media image is a positive and accurate reflection of their unique personality and brand.

CHAPTER FOURTEEN

Understanding Legal Aspects

While your pet's Instagram journey is filled with fun and adorable moments, there are legal aspects to consider. This chapter will guide you through some of the important legal issues, such as copyright laws regarding pet photography, contracts for sponsored content, and how to protect your pet's image rights.

Understanding Copyright Issues Related to Pet Photography

When sharing and creating content for your pet's social media platforms, it's crucial to respect copyright laws to avoid legal issues and maintain ethical practices. Here's how to navigate copyright considerations:

1. Your Original Content: When you take photos and videos of your pet, you automatically own the copyright to that content. This means you have the exclusive right to use, reproduce, and distribute the content. However, it's essential to be aware that once you post your content on social media platforms, you may be granting the platform certain rights to use and display your content as per their terms of service.

Protect your original content by watermarking your photos or adding copyright notices where appropriate. This can discourage others from using your content without permission. If someone wants to use your pet's content, always ensure you give explicit permission and determine how it will be used and credited.

2. Others' Content: If you want to share someone else's photo or video on your pet's account, always obtain permission from the original content owner. This applies to content found on other social media accounts, websites,

or anywhere else on the internet. Respect the creator's rights and wishes by reaching out for their consent before reposting.

When sharing others' content, make sure to credit the original owner appropriately. Provide proper attribution by mentioning the creator's name or username, and ideally, link back to their original post or profile.

3. Music and Art: Using copyrighted music, artwork, or other copyrighted materials in your pet's content requires special consideration. Copyright holders have exclusive rights to control the use of their works, and unauthorized use can lead to copyright infringement claims.

If you want to use copyrighted music, consider obtaining licenses or using royalty-free music from reputable sources. Many platforms provide libraries of royalty-free music that you can use without infringing on copyright.

Always be cautious about using content that you do not have explicit permission to use or that might infringe on someone else's copyright. Respecting copyright laws not only keeps you legally compliant but also shows respect for other content creators and fosters a positive online community for your pet's brand.

Navigating Contracts and Agreements for Sponsored Content

As a pet influencer, sponsored content deals can be exciting opportunities to collaborate with brands and monetize your pet's platform. However, it's crucial to handle contracts with care to protect your interests and maintain ethical practices. Here's how to approach sponsored content contracts:

1. Understand the Terms: Before signing any contract, carefully review and understand all the terms and conditions. Look for essential details such as payment terms, deliverables, timelines, exclusivity clauses (if any), and content rights.

Pay close attention to the scope of work and what is expected of you as an influencer. Understand the requirements for content creation, posting frequency, and any guidelines or restrictions provided by the brand. Be sure you are comfortable with these terms before proceeding.

2. Get Legal Help: When dealing with contracts, it's always advisable to seek legal advice from a lawyer experienced in influencer marketing or contract law. A lawyer can help you fully understand the implications of the contract and ensure that your rights and interests are protected.

If you have concerns or questions about specific clauses, a lawyer can help you negotiate better terms and advocate on your behalf. Having legal support can give you peace of mind and help you make informed decisions about sponsored content partnerships.

3. Fulfill Your Obligations: Once you have signed the contract, it's essential to fulfill your contractual obligations diligently. This includes creating and posting content as per the agreement, meeting deadlines, and maintaining transparency with your followers about sponsored content.

Strive to produce high-quality content that aligns with your pet's brand and the brand you're collaborating with. Be open and honest with your audience about sponsored content, using appropriate disclosure statements as required by law and platform policies.

Remember that sponsored content contracts are legally binding agreements, and it's crucial to approach them with professionalism and diligence. By understanding the terms, seeking legal advice, and fulfilling your contractual obligations, you can navigate sponsored content partnerships successfully while maintaining your pet's authenticity and credibility with your audience.

Protecting Your Pet's Image Rights

As your pet's fame grows, protecting their image rights becomes increasingly important to safeguard their brand and prevent unauthorized use. Here's how to ensure your pet's image is protected:

1. Trademarking: Consider trademarking your pet's name, logo, or any unique taglines associated with their brand. A trademark registration provides legal protection and prevents others from using similar names or logos for commercial purposes without your permission.

Consult with a trademark attorney to navigate the registration process and ensure your pet's brand is properly protected. Trademarking can help you establish a strong brand identity for your pet and prevent potential confusion with other pet accounts or products.

2. Unauthorized Use: Keep a vigilant eye on the internet and social media platforms for any unauthorized use of your pet's image or content. If you come across instances of unauthorized use, consult with an attorney experienced in intellectual property rights to determine the best course of action.

Depending on the severity of the unauthorized use, your attorney may advise sending a cease and desist letter to the responsible party, requesting them to remove the content or cease using your pet's image immediately. In more serious cases, legal action, such as filing a lawsuit for copyright or trademark infringement, may be necessary to protect your pet's image rights.

3. Privacy: As your pet gains more fame, it's essential to maintain a certain level of privacy for their well-being and safety. Be cautious about sharing sensitive information, such as your home address or personal details, that could put your pet at risk.

While sharing aspects of your pet's life is part of being a pet influencer, strike a balance between providing an authentic connection with your audience and safeguarding your pet's privacy. Consider focusing on the positive aspects of their journey and avoiding content that could attract unwanted attention or potential risks.

Protecting your pet's image rights is crucial for maintaining their reputation and brand integrity as they gain fame as a pet influencer. By trademarking their name and logo, addressing unauthorized use, and respecting their privacy, you can ensure your pet's image is safeguarded while they continue to bring joy and inspiration to their growing audience.

While the legal aspects may seem overwhelming, understanding and addressing them is essential to protect you and your pet. Remember, it's always wise to consult with legal professionals when in doubt or faced with complex legal issues.

Conclusion

As we conclude this book, we take a moment to reflect on the journey we've embarked on together. Becoming a pet influencer isn't merely about the fame or the potential income. It's a celebration of your pet's unique personality, the joy they bring into your life, and the ability to share that joy with a wider community. This chapter will guide you through reflecting on your pet's Instagram journey, celebrating your achievements and milestones, and continuing to share your pet's unique story with the world.

Reflecting on Your Pet's Instagram Journey

Reflecting on Your Pet's Instagram Journey

Looking back at your pet's Instagram journey can be a heartwarming and enlightening experience. Take a moment to acknowledge how far you and your beloved companion have come and the meaningful impact your journey has had on both of your lives:

1. Journey: Remember the humble beginnings of your pet's Instagram account, from that very first photo you excitedly posted. Reflect on the growth and development of your pet's brand, as you navigated the world of social media and discovered what resonated with your audience.

Consider the special moments captured in photos and videos, the milestones celebrated, and the connections formed with followers who have become a part of your pet's extended community. Embrace the memories of the joy and laughter your pet has brought to others through their unique personality and charm.

2. Challenges and Growth: Recall the challenges you faced along the way - from figuring out the best content strategy to managing unexpected hurdles. Reflect on how you overcame these challenges, learning valuable lessons and developing resilience in the process.

Your journey as a pet influencer has likely been a journey of growth and personal development as well. The dedication and hard work you put into managing your pet's account have likely contributed to your growth as an individual, social media manager, and pet owner.

3. Meaning: Consider what this journey means to both you and your pet. Has it brought you closer as you embarked on this adventure together? Has your pet's Instagram presence enriched their life, providing them with new experiences, love, and opportunities?

Your pet's Instagram journey may have positively impacted not only your pet but also others in the pet-loving community. The smiles, support, and inspiration your pet brings to their followers may have a profound and lasting effect, reminding everyone of the beauty and joy that pets can bring into our lives.

As you reflect on this remarkable journey, celebrate the love, connection, and growth you and your pet have experienced. Embrace the joy of sharing your pet's unique brand with the world and the meaningful impact it has had on the lives of others. The bond you have formed with your furry companion and the lasting memories created through this social media journey are something to cherish and be grateful for as you continue to embark on new adventures together.

Celebrating Your Achievements and Milestones

Celebrating your pet's Instagram accomplishments is a wonderful way to appreciate the journey and recognize the positive impact it has had on both you and your pet. Here's how to embrace and commemorate the milestones, both big and small:

1. Milestones: Take a moment to celebrate the significant milestones your pet's Instagram account has achieved. Whether it's reaching a particular follower count, hitting a new engagement record, or securing a successful brand collaboration, each achievement is a testament to your dedication and creativity.

Share your excitement with your followers, thanking them for their support and being an integral part of your pet's journey. Milestones are not just numbers; they represent the joy and love your pet brings to their community and the connections you've formed along the way.

2. Small Victories: Cherish the small victories that may not be as quantifiable but are equally meaningful. Celebrate the posts that touched the hearts of your followers, the comments that brought a smile to your face, or the moments when your pet's unique personality shone through.

Remember that these seemingly small triumphs are what build the foundation of your pet's relationship with their audience. They foster a sense of community and make your followers feel connected and engaged, ultimately contributing to the authenticity and success of your pet's brand.

3. Personal Growth: Acknowledge and celebrate the personal growth you've experienced as a pet influencer. Reflect on the skills you've acquired in content creation, social media management, and marketing. Recognize the relationships you've formed with fellow pet influencers, brands, and your supportive audience.

Your pet's Instagram journey is not just about their fame; it's about the growth and development it has sparked in you. Embrace the learning opportunities and the chance to explore your creativity and passion for pets and photography.

Taking time to celebrate your pet's Instagram accomplishments is a way of expressing gratitude for the joys and challenges that have shaped your journey. It's a reminder to treasure the meaningful connections you've made and to continue spreading joy and inspiration through your pet's unique brand. So, celebrate every achievement, big or small, and cherish the love and impact your pet brings to the world through their social media presence.

Continuing to Share Your Pet's Unique Story with the World

The conclusion of this book isn't the end of your pet's Instagram journey. It's just the beginning:

1. Consistency: The key to sustaining your pet's Instagram success is to remain consistent in your efforts. Stay true to the essence of why you started this journey - the love and passion you have for your pet. Let that passion shine through in every post, connecting with your audience on a deeper level.

Your followers appreciate the authenticity and dedication you bring to your pet's account. Continue to share content consistently, whether it's heartwarming stories, entertaining tricks, or candid moments that showcase your pet's unique personality.

2. Innovation: Instagram is a dynamic platform with ever-changing trends and features. Embrace the spirit of innovation and keep your content fresh and engaging. Explore new content formats, experiment with different ideas, and adapt to the latest trends.

Your pet's Instagram journey should reflect the evolving tastes and preferences of your audience. Stay curious and open to trying new things, always finding creative ways to showcase your pet's brand and captivate your followers.

3. Purpose: Throughout your pet's Instagram journey, always stay grounded in your purpose - sharing your pet's unique story. Remember that each post is an opportunity to bring joy, laughter, and inspiration to someone's day.

Regardless of the number of followers you have, never lose sight of the impact your pet's Instagram account can have on the lives of others. Whether it's a heartwarming moment that brightens someone's day or a meaningful message that resonates with your audience, each post contributes to the magic of your pet's social media presence.

As you continue on this enchanting journey, cherish the memories you've created, the connections you've formed, and the love you've shared with your beloved companion. Your pet's Instagram account is not just a virtual presence but a reflection of the beautiful bond between you and your furry friend. So, go forth with passion, innovation, and purpose, knowing that the story of your pet's Instagram journey is far from over - it's only just begun. The world eagerly awaits to see more of your pet's captivating tale unfold!

As you wrap up this book, remember that you're not just an owner—you're your pet's biggest fan, and their most passionate storyteller. The story of your pet's Instagram journey doesn't end here; instead, it unfolds every day, one post at a time. So, continue to share, celebrate, and above all, enjoy the wonderful journey of your pet's Instagram stardom.